Helion & Company Limited
Unit 8 Amherst Business Centre
Budbrooke Road
Warwick
CV34 5WE
England
Tel. 01926 499 619
Email: info@helion.co.uk
Website: www.helion.co.uk
Twitter: @helionbooks
Visit our blog http://blog.helion.co.uk/

Text © Stephen Rookes 2022
Colour artwork © David Bocquelet, Helion &
    Company and Tom Cooper 2022
Maps drawn by George Anderson © Helion
    & Company 2022 and Tom Cooper 2022
Photographs © as individually credited

Designed & typeset by Farr out Publications,
    Wokingham, Berkshire
Cover design by Paul Hewitt, Battlefield
    Design (www.battlefield-design.co.uk)

ISBN 978-1-915070-54-8

British Library Cataloguing-in-Publication
    Data
A catalogue record for this book is available
    from the British Library

We always welcome receiving book
proposals from prospective authors.

Contents

Acronyms and Abbreviations   2
Acknowledgements   2
Introduction   2

1   The *Force Publique* in the Congo Free State: Origins and Structure   3
2   Military Challenges to the Congo Free State   15
3   The *Force Publique*, 1908–1918   23
4   The Interwar Period: The Development of the Belgian Congo   35
5   The Belgian Congo and the Second World War   40
6   Aviation in the Belgian Congo, 1940–1944   45
7   Trouble Brews in the Belgian Congo   70
8   Belgium's Military Response to Civil Disorder in the Congo,
         1959–1960   76

Bibliography   88
Notes   90
About the Author   96

Note: In order to simplify the use of this book, all names, locations and geographic designations are as provided in *The Times World Atlas*, or other traditionally accepted major sources of reference, as of the time of described events. Correspondingly, the term 'Congo' designates the area of the former Belgian colony of the Congo Free State, granted independence as the Democratic Republic of the Congo in June 1960 and in use until 1971 when the country was renamed Republic of Zaire, which, in turn, reverted to Democratic Republic of the Congo in 1997, and which remains in use today. As such, Congo is not to be mistaken for the former French colony of Middle Congo (Moyen Congo), officially named the Republic of the Congo on its independence in August 1960, also known as Congo-Brazzaville.

Dedication

This volume is dedicated to the memory of Michèle Timmermans-Zoll (1940–2019),
shot while a hostage of Simba rebels, Stanleyville, 24 November 1964.
Que son âme repose en paix.

Acronyms and Abbreviations

ABAKO	*Alliance des Bakongo*		**GEA**	German East Africa
ABIR	Anglo-Belgian India Rubber Company		**KAR**	King's African Rifles
ANC	*Armée Nationale Congolaise* (Congolese National Army)		**LARA**	*Ligne Aérienne du Roi Albert*
			Lt.	Lieutenant
BAF	Belgian Air Force		**MDAP**	Mutual Defense Assistance Program (US)
BAKA	*Base Aérienne Katanga*		**MNC**	*Mouvement National Congolais*
BALUBAKAT	*Association Générale des Baluba de Katanga*		**NCO**	Non-commissioned Officer
Cdt.	Commandant (Major)		**NRP**	Northern Rhodesian Police
CEHC	*Comité d'Etudes du Haut-Congo*		**OTU**	Operational Training Unit
CENAC	*Comité d'Etudes pour la Navigation Aérienne au Congo*		**RAF**	Royal Air Force
			RATG	Rhodesian Air Training Group
CFS	Congo Free State		**SAAF**	South African Air Force
CIA	Central Intelligence Agency		**SABENA**	*Société Anonyme Belge d'Exploitation de la Navigation Aérienne*
Cométro	*Commandement supérieur des forces métropolitaines d'Afrique*		**SGB**	*Société Générale de Belgique*
CONAKAT	*Confédération des associations tribales du Katanga*		**SNETA**	*Syndicat Nationale pour l'Etude des Transports Aériens*
DFC	Distinguished Flying Cross		**Ss. Lt**	*Sous-Lieutenant* (Second Lieutenant)
EPA	*Ecole de Pilotage Avancée* (Belgian Congo)		**Ss-officier**	*Sous-officier* (NCO)
FAC	*Force Aérienne Congolaise* (Congolese Air Force)		**UMHK**	*Union Minière du Haut-Katanga*
FAF	*Flight Appui Feu* (Fire Assistance Flights)		**UNOC**	United Nations Operations Congo
FAK	*Force Aérienne Katangaise* (Katanga Air Force)		**USAAF**	United States Army Air Force
FP	*Force Publique*		**WAC**	West Africa Command

Acknowledgements

The completion of this volume would not have been possible without the assistance and encouragement of the following people. Daniel Brackx kindly gave his permission for the use of a large quantity of photos taken from his website https://www.belgian-wings.be/. A highly informative website, Daniel Brackx is an authority on the history of the Belgian Air Force. Secondly, I would like to thank Colonel Polydore Stevens of the Belgian Air Force. Born in the Belgian Congo, he has directed me towards numerous sources. I look forward to working alongside him in the writing of the second volume in this series, *Belgian Military Forces in the Congo: The Force Aérienne Tactique Congo (FATAC), 1964–1967.*

Introduction

The *Force Publique* was a paramilitary gendarmerie given official status in 1885 by King Léopold II of Belgium. Serving to maintain public order and to protect Léopold's commercial interests from Arab traders and the ambitions of other European colonising nations, the existence of the *Force Publique* lasted until July 1960 and its replacement by the *Armée Nationale Congolaise*. Tracing the history of the *Force Publique* from its inception to its conclusion, this volume complements two previously published volumes dealing with the political and military events leading up to, and during, the Congo Crisis. Namely *Ripe for Rebellion: Political and Military Insurgency in the Congo, 1946–1964*, and *For God and the CIA: Cuban Exile Forces in the Congo and Beyond, 1959–1967*, the current volume precedes a second volume dealing with Belgian military forces in the Congo. A military history of the *Force Publique* as well as, to some extent, a social history of the Congo Free State and the Belgian Congo, the intention of this volume is to describe not only the military campaigns against the aforementioned Arab traders, but also to examine in detail the participation of Belgian forces in the East African Campaigns of the First and Second World Wars. These parts leading the volume to extend its main centre of interest to the military operations of Britain, France, Germany, South Africa,

Southern Rhodesia and Northern Rhodesia in East Africa, later chapters focus on the construction of a colonial air force and Belgian civil and military aviation in the Congo. Of particular interest, then, to aviation enthusiasts, the large quantity maps, graphs, and photos contained in this volume will benefit anyone seeking to increase their knowledge of the Congo and the Congolese people. Effectively, and similarly to several colonial armies, the rank and file of the *Force Publique* comprised Congolese conscripts and volunteers.

1

The *Force Publique* in the Congo Free State: Origins and Structure

The Portuguese navigator Diego Cão, employed by King John II to take up the voyages of discovery made by Henry the Navigator in the fifteenth century, in around 1482, thus native of Vila Real became the first European to set eyes on the mouth of the River Congo and to explore the coasts of Gabon and the current day Namibia. Should Cão have continued his journey into the heartlands of the Congo, he would have discovered a large variety of different contours and

topography. Ranging from snow-topped mountains and volcanoes such as the Blue Mountains in the northeast of the Congo, the Eastern Rift Mountains in the Great Lakes region to luxuriant savannas, mosquito-infested swamps and dense rainforests that covered much of the land, Cão would have also discovered up to 15 cultural regions and over 250 different ethnic groups living side-by-side. Mainly residing in the thousands of small settlements that

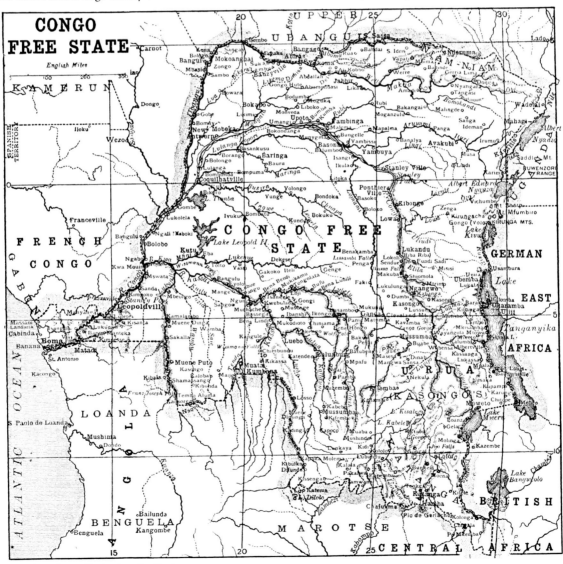

Map of the Congo Free State. (Author's collection)

A representation of Stanley's meeting with David Livingstone at Ujiji in 1871. (Science Photo Library)

were dotted across the landscape, communities such as the Balunda, Baluba, Bakongo or Batwa peoples spoke a variety of dialects belonging to the Sudanic, Nigritic or Bantu languages, the latter the most widely used. Polygamy and cannibalism were common in these hunter-gatherer societies ruled by village chiefs respecting traditions and customs passed down over hundreds of years.

One of the earliest examples of how small, localised societies grew into much larger and more powerful entities is that of the Kingdom of the Kongo. Ruled by the Kikongo-speaking House of Kilukeni since the end of the fourteenth century, the existence of the kingdom came about through an alliance of the Mpenba Kasi and the Mbata tribes.[1] The kingdom covered areas of western Congo and parts of current day northern Angola and activities were centred on its capital Mbanza Kongo, later named San Salvador by the Portuguese. A significant preoccupation for rulers of the kingdom such as Henrique I Nerika a Mpudi or King Alvaro I was ensuring that the lands it occupied remained safe from attack from rival kingdoms. Examples that serve to illustrate this type of attack are the wars against the Bateke from the neighbouring Anziku Kingdom[2] or the invasion of the Jaga which took place shortly after Alvaro came to the throne in 1567. The latter was the most serious assault on Kikongo authority as the Jaga managed to capture San Salvador and badly disrupt an economic activity on which the kingdom had thrived since its inception, i.e., slavery.

The kingdom's trade in human commodity had increased gradually through its ability to defeat its rivals in battle and to use those captured as slaves. However, once the Portuguese became involved from 1511, and huge financial gains could be made as demand for slaves developed, forays were carried out into the rural regions surrounding the kingdom to fuel their needs. Up to 1789, 6–8 million people were transported from the ports of the Lower Congo.[3] As the success of larger Congolese societies had become increasingly dependent on this lucrative trade, it comes as no surprise to learn that their downfall coincided with Britain's abolition of the slave trade in 1839 and its sinking of ships seen to be carrying human cargo. This was the case, at least, in western areas of the Congo. In the centre and east of the country the slave trade continued well into the 1890s with the Kazembe, Kuba and Lunda kingdoms growing powerful due to their business relations with Arab traders who had crossed the land from Khartoum in the Sudan or from Dar es Salaam in modern-day Tanzania. While large parts of the Kikongo kingdom would be integrated into northern Angola in the early nineteenth century, the gradual disappearance of the slave trade meant that its inhabitants had to find other means of making a living. Fortunately, other European nations seeking trading opportunities were to make their appearance in the Congo shortly after.

As geographical and botanical societies began to wonder what unknown lands and species lay beyond the coastal regions of the Congo, in 1816, the British admiralty gave Captain James Tuckey the mission of investigating whether there was a link between the Congo and Niger basins of western and central Africa. Though this mission aboard the aptly named HMS *Congo* ended when Tuckey and his crew died from fevers and attacks by natives, the publication of his notes in 1818 aroused much interest for wealthy individuals like Sir Joseph Banks, the President of the Royal Society who were prepared to sponsor further expeditions. A founding member of the Association for Promoting the Discovery of the Interior Parts of Africa, also known as the African Association, and a participant in Captain James Cook's first great voyage (1768–1771), Banks is

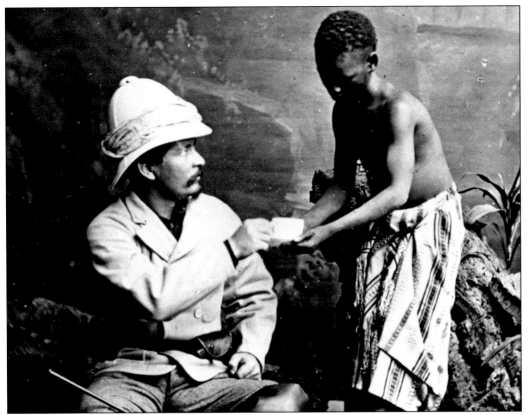

Born as John Rowlands in Wales, Henry Stanley is known for his exploration of the Nile and Congo Rivers under the aegis of King Léopold II of Belgium. (New Statesman)

King Léopold II of Belgium (1835–1907) became Belgium's second king in 1865. First taking an interest in the commercial possibilities offered in central Africa, Léopold II became the absolute ruler of the Congo Free State after the Berlin Conference (1884–1885). (World.Time.com)

often credited as one of the initiators of a period known as the age of African exploration.[4] Dedicated to the exploration of West Africa, finding the source of the Niger River, and discovering Timbuktu, Mali's lost 'city of gold', Scottish missionaries such as Robert Moffat (1795–1883) and his son-in-law David Livingstone (1813–1873) led the way in the anthropological study of the peoples that inhabited more southerly and central regions of the African continent. Though the Portuguese already ensconced in west-central Africa, the Dutch having settled in South Africa as early as 1652, and Arab slave traders among the few that had ventured inwards into Africa from the east, much of the area that lay in between remained unexplored and unseen by anyone not a member of the indigenous tribes or who had been part of the Bantu expansion from the north to the south of Africa, a movement that continued into the seventeenth century.

Having ventured northwards from South Africa into the Bantu-speaking lands of the Matabele in current day Zimbabwe, Moffat was keen that Livingstone should explore the lands that lie to the north of Bechuanaland where no missionary had ever been. In 1854, under the service of the London Missionary Society (LMS) Livingstone embarked on a two-year-long voyage that would take him from Quelimane in Mozambique to Luanda in Angola. The first European to cross central Africa at that latitude, Livingstone discovered the existence of the Mosi-o-Tunya which he renamed Victoria Falls in honour of the British queen. Then, on the advice of fellow explorers, Richard Burton (1821–1890) and John Hanning Speke (1827–1864), Livingstone made further headway into the interior of the Congo and was even able to explore the Congo's Kasai River as well as some of its tributaries. During subsequent expeditions, Livingstone discovered two other lakes in the Congo – Mweru and Bangweulu – and on his final expedition (1866–1873) he travelled up the Lualaba River also in search of the source of the Nile. Travelling to Ujiji in what was then Tanganyika in 1871, it was here that Henry Morton Stanley is said to have uttered the immortal words, "Dr. Livingstone, I presume".

The accounts of the explorers' different journeys into the heart of Africa told of the immense quantities of mineral riches which were to be found in Katanga in the southeast of the Congo.[5] Its history of mining dating back over 1,000 years,[6] the region was reputed all over central Africa for its source of copper long before the arrival of Europeans.[7] This metal was taken from the Katanga in the shape of St. Andrew's crosses, rings, axes, lances and different ornaments by Arab and black Portuguese traders and it was taken from the interior to the ports which lie on the shores of the Indian and Atlantic oceans. Indeed, in *The Last Journals* published in 1874, Livingstone was to describe how he came across a caravan of Arab traders near Lake Mweruthat carrying more than five tons of copper such was its value.[8] Other European explorers followed in Livingstone's footsteps. England's Verney Lovett Cameron, Scotland's Joseph Thomson – the geologist who inspired Haggard's *King Solomon's Mines* – and the German Hermann Wissman were all to mention traces of gold in accounts of their travels. As well as catching the attention of the public, the accounts also sparked the interest of King Léopold II of Belgium, a head of state keen to exploit the commercial and philanthropic opportunities on offer in lands yet to be claimed by other European colonial powers.

To advance his project, in 1876 Léopold sent invitations to the leading geographical societies in Europe requesting their representation at what became the Brussels Geographic Conference. Held from 12–14 September of that year, Léopold explained in his opening address how important it was to eliminate the Arab slave trade in Africa and how much the African would benefit from an input of European culture and trading methods. One way by which this 'civilising project' could be implemented on a practical level was through the setting up of a number of stations across Africa that could be used by scientists and explorers as bases as they carried out their work. Supported by attendees of the conference such as the explorers Cameron, James Augustus Grant, Gustav Nachtigal, or Friedrich Rohlfs who provided some of the specifics of the operation, the International Commission for the Exploration and Civilisation of Central Africa decided that four such stations should be established and that a newly created International African Association (IAA) should be put in charge of their implementation and governance. Nevertheless, whereas national committees were then established to further the plan and to provide its funding, within two years countries such as Austria, Italy, Portugal, Germany or the United States appeared to be focusing on individual national objectives rather than international collaboration as regards Africa. Great Britain's Royal Geographical Society, for example, decided that it could not, by its constitution, "enter upon any field of operations other than that of exploration". It believed that it might eventually make a financial contribution to the International Commission, but resolved that the best course of action was to set up a national fund called the "African Exploration Fund", a fund "devoted to the scientific examination of Africa, the physical features and resources, the best routes to the interior, and all such matters as may be instrumental in preparing the way for opening up Africa by peaceful means".[9]

Despite this type of financial rebuttal, Léopold pressed ahead with his plans by using a separate entity he created in November 1878 called the *Comité d'Etudes du Haut-Congo* (CEHC), or Committee for the Study of the Upper Congo. A committee whose object was to "penetrate barbarous Africa by ascending the Congo river" and "to seek practicable means of establishing regular communications along the Upper and Lower Congo", it sought "to create amicable relations for commercial purposes with the tribes that dwelt in the interior" in order to offer them the "varied productions of European industry".[10] Léopold subsequently dispatched Stanley to the Congo to sign a number of agreements with different Congolese district chiefs therefore making philanthropic and scientific ends indistinguishable from political objectives. The Treaty of Vivi (1880) signed in June 1880, for example, saw the cession of territory and the transfer of sovereignty to the CEHC. Similar agreements such as the Treaty of Manyanga (1882), or the Treaty of Léopoldville (1883) meant that huge areas of central Africa were designated to become part of a commercially based independent state in the heart of Africa. The CEHC then becoming the *Association Internationale*

The *Roi des Belges* was just one of the steamships used to ferry explorers along the Congo's network of rivers. This steamship is particular in that it carried Polish-English writer Joseph Conrad up the Congo River in 1889. Conrad's fictionalisation of his journey into the interior of the Congo entitled *The Heart of Darkness* served as inspiration for *Apocalypse Now*, Francis Ford Coppola's epic dealing with the Vietnam War. (Author's collection)

du Congo (AIC), or the International Association of the Congo, in April and November 1884, the AIC was recognised by the United States and Germany respectively. Shortly after, a conference was opened in Berlin "to regulate, in amicable spirit and with cordiality, the conditions that could assure the development of the commerce of the Congo, and arrange for the prevention of errors and mutual misunderstandings".[11] Prince Otto von Bismark thus conferring outright authority of the now Congo Independent State (CIS) to Léopold II, in August 1885 the Belgian king then sought the approbation of his government to formalise relations between Belgium and the Congo on a purely personal level. Henceforth, the Congo Independent State or the Congo Free State would be free from any legal procedures relative to Belgian law leaving Léopold II to govern as he wished.

With the Berlin Conference (1884–1885) seeing the African continent divided up and shared by European powers and with Léopold finding himself in control of an area roughly 77 times larger than Belgium, the commercial success of the Congo Free State and its future as an independent entity relied on not only the continuation of the drawing up of trading agreements in the Congo's different tribal areas, but also insuring that encroachments across roughly

Table 1: Rank and file foreign recruitment into the Force Publique, 1893–1901[18]

Origin	1883	1884	1885	1886	1887	1888	1889	1890	1891	1892
Liberia	-	-	-	-	-	143	168		30	59
Abyssinia	-	-	-	-	-	-	-	-	-	412
Egypt	-	-	-	-	-	-	-	217	1	-
Dahomey	-	-	-	-	-	-	185	-	-	1
Zanzibar	-	-	-	-	-	783	-	243	-	-
Nigeria	50	30	20	5	662	305	15	1,253	548	316
Sierra Leone	-	-	-	-	-	-	204	-	9	138
Total	50	30	20	5	662	1,231	572	1,713	597	926

Origin	1893	1894	1895	1896	1897	1898	1899	1900	1901	Total
Liberia	99	89	12	5	38	20	11	17	8	708
Gold Coast	192	295	36	5	12	21	20	6	4	591
Abyssinia	-	-	-	-	-	-	-	-	-	412
Somalia	215	-	-	-	-	-	-	-	-	215
Egypt	-	-	-	1	1	1	1	1	-	223
Dahomey	-	-	-	5	3	-	2	1	1	198
Zanzibar	593		32	109		2	8	2	3	1,775
Nigeria	463	774	340	328	76	211	111	37	41	5,585
Sierra Leone	793	715	92	176	98	237	128	85	70	2,745
Total	2,355	1,873	512	629	228	492	281	149	127	12,452

defined borders were quickly dealt with so that French, British and Portuguese ambitions of territorial advancement were quickly subdued. Even before the Berlin Conference Léopold's agents were thus dispatched to throughout what was believed to be the extent of the Congo Free State to establish and secure more defined areas of as well as making voyages of discovery along the Congo's network of waterways. While the map near the beginning of this chapter shows the extent of the Congo Free State *circa* 1895, many of these voyages were sponsored by the Upper Congo Study Committee of the Military Cartographic Institute. Given the nature of their sponsor, unsurprisingly a number of soldiers turned explorers were among those willing to make the journey into still unknown lands. Former soldier and colonial administrator Edmond-Winnie-Victor Hanssens (1843–1884), for example, reached Banana in March 1882. A small seaport situated on the Atlantic coast at the extreme tip of territory still under Congolese control, Hanssens

was joined by Lieutenant Joseph Vandevelde (1855–1882), Théodore Nilis (1851–1905), and Nicolas Grang (1854–1883), a Luxembourger soldier.[12] The dates of the explorers are testament to the harsh conditions in which these discoveries were made: all four making their way up the River Congo to Vivi along with Captain Grant-Elliot, Hanssens, Vandevelde and Grang all died from tropical illnesses contracted along the way. They had, nevertheless, been able to hoist the flag of the Congo Free State to ward off French claims to areas north of the River Congo led by Pierre de Brazza. Featuring a yellow star on a blue background, the flag reputedly designed by Stanley forms the basis of the current Congolese flag. American participation in the evolution also came through the voyages of Paul-Amédée Le Marinel. Although born to French parents, Le Marinel was born in Long Grove, Iowa in 1858, before returning to Belgium in 1876. Seconded to the Military Cartographic Institute, Le Marinel was sent to Luluabourg in the Kasai in 1885 and along with Alexandre Delcommune (1855–1922) explored the areas around the Sankuru and Lubefu rivers.[13] As well as helping lay the foundations for Léopold's private state in the Congo, Thédore Nilis, Delcommune and Le Marinel became important figures in the setting up of the Free State's armed forces, the *Force Publique* (FP).

The presence of the FP, a gendarmerie and paramilitary force established in 1885, was necessary not only to protect Léopold's interests from the aspirations of Germany to the east, the British to the south, and the French to the north, but also to provide protection from tribal movements and bands of Arab slave and ivory traders opposing Léopold's rule. This was a common feature of time no more epitomised by the 32 attacks from local tribes repulsed by Stanley as he made his way from Nyangwe in Maniema and Stanley Pool (now Pool Malebo) in the mid-1870s.[14] Assisted in this task by Zanzibari porters, Stanley soon realised that he would require armed protection if he hoped to prevent further attacks. The origins of the FP dating back to the arming of porters, West African mercenaries were also recruited to fulfil security duties, and by 1884 natives of Cabinda (Angolan enclave), Ethiopians, Somalians, Egyptians had also been recruited to bolster numbers.[15]

Table 2: Scandinavian NCOs and Officers recruited to serve in the *Force Publique*, 1878–1904[19]

Origin	NCOs	Officers	Total
Sweden	18	47	65
Norway	3	26	29
Denmark	4	53	57
Total	25	126	151

Notes: One source gives the total number of Scandinavian officers as 126 (53 Danes, 47 Swedes, 26 Norwegians). The same source states that 648 Belgians, 112 Italians also served as officers as well as a small number of US and UK citizens.[20] Between 1878 and 1904, four Swedish and two Danish officers were killed in action while 24 Swedes, 10 Norwegians and 20 Danes succumbed to illness. A total of 12 Swiss citizens served as officers (9) or NCOs (3). One Swiss officer was killed in action.

Table 3: Conscription of Congolese into the *Force Publique* 1895–1914[21]

Territory, district, or zone	1892	1893	1894	1895	1896	1897	1898	1899	1900	1901	1902	1903
Banana	-	-	-	-	-	-	-	-	-	-	25	50
Boma-Mayumbe	300	370	350	270	400	400	125	75	50	200	25	50
Matadi	-	-	-	-	-	-	-	-	-	-	75	100
Cataractes	120	120	100	100	100	100	75	50	100	75	-	-
Stanley Pool	180	100	100	100	100	100	75	50	50	50	75	100
Kwango	120	120	120	200	200	200	75	25	40	50	50	50
Lake Léopold II	-	-	-	-	100	100	150	150	50	75	75	150
Equateur	180	200	200	300	600	600	450	200	250	300	300	250
Bangala and Mongala	300	300	300	300	300	300	550	250	250	300	250	250
Ubangi	180	300	600	350	500	500	150	150	150	300	200	350
Aruwimi	180	250	280	200	300	300	300	150	150	150	200	200
Lualaba Kasai	300	1,050	500	600	800	800	150	75	-	-	300	500

Territory, District, or Zone	1904	1905	1906	1907	1908	1909	1910	1911	1912	1913	1914
Banana and Boma-Mayumbe	-	25	30	30	20	31	49	-	-	-	-
Matadi and Cataractes	-	50	65	50	25	31	46	100	100	73	80
Stanley Pool and Kwango	-	100	130	75	40	63	155	-	-	-	-
Lake Léopold II	-	90	120	170	85	134	230	205	205	144	260
Equateur	-	250	325	275	140	212	338	325	379	211	160
Bangala and Mongala	-	250	325	400	230	181	464	473	544	287	300
Ubangi	-	210	275	220	100	142	233	225	225	127	125
Aruwimi	-	250	325	270	125	157	237	215	257	139	150
Lualuba Kasai	-	430	560	500	250	252	286	302	352	200	200

Notes: 11,970 men were recruited from the Rubi-Uele, Makua, Uele-Bomu, Makrakra, and the Lado Enclave (from 1907). Administrative reorganisation in 1910 led to all these districts forming the Uele Province. Similarly, from 1907 over 10,400 men from Haut-Ituri, Stanley Falls, Ponthierville and Maniema were recruited following the integration of these districts into the Oriente Province. 428 men were recruited from the Ruzizi-Kivu district while a further 405 came from Katanga from 1910. From 1895 to 1914, the annual conscription of Congolese men amounted to some 2,997. From 1895 there was a sharp fall in the number of foreign recruits into the *Force Publique*. This is due to a decree issued by Léopold II in 1891. From July 1891, the Congolese were subject to an annual conscription (levée). Up to 1914, some 66,340 men from all areas of the Congo served to prop up the Congo Free State and, from 1908, the Belgian Congo.

Once recruited, men were sent to garrisons in various parts of the Congo Free State. Indeed, according to Camille Coquilhat, another Belgian soldier and explorer, of the 30 men who made up forces in New Antwerp (then Bangala, then Makanza), two came from Cabinda, 17 came from Zanzibar, and 11 were Hausa warriors.[16] Of the Tanzanians, three came from the region of Ounyamouezi, one came from the Comoros Islands, and four came from western areas. The last came from Maniema and had formerly been made a slave by the Arabs. Among the Hausa recruited in Lagos and in the Ivory Coast, two were true Hausas while nine were members of Nigeria's Yoruba nation.[17] As shown in the accompanying tables, from 1888 the recruitment of mercenaries making up the rank and file, non-commissioned officers and officers of the FP was widespread (see Table 1). While we note that over 151 Scandinavians were recruited to serve as officers (see Table 2), we also note that there was a fall off

in the number of recruits from 1895. This coincided with an effort to recruit more native Congolese into the force. Locally conscripted soldiers became known as Askaris. They played a crucial role in upholding Belgian authority as local recruits did in other European colonies in sub-Saharan Africa, particularly in the Great Lakes region, northeast Africa, and central Africa.

The term *"Force Publique"* first mentioned in an 1885 statute relative to the organisation of the central government,[23] from a statutory point of view the CFS's armed forces served under the overall command of a Governor General (GG),[24] with the day-to-day activities of these forces overseen by a District Commissioner.[25] Its creation not officialised until a decree of August 1888,[26] Commanders-in-chief (see Table 4), were placed under the authority of the District Commissioner, and were responsible for the "discipline, training, feeding and outfitting of the troops" under

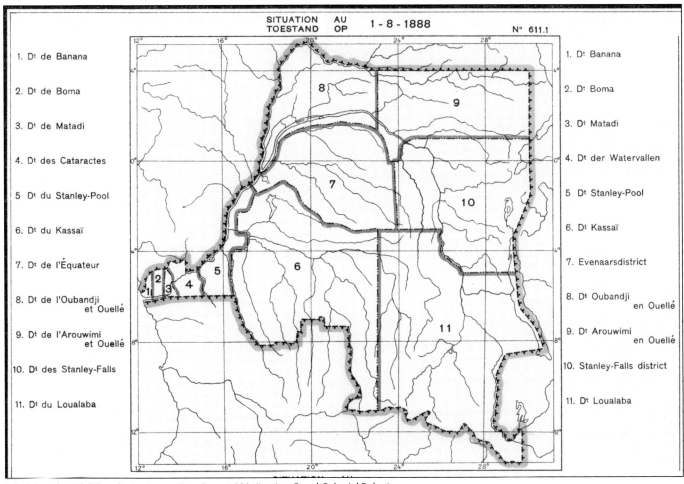

Administrative Divisions in the Congo Free State, 1888. (Institut Royal Colonial Belge)

1. Dᵗ de Banana
2. Dᵗ de Boma
3. Dᵗ de Matadi
4. Dᵗ des Cataractes
5. Dᵗ du Stanley-Pool
6. Dᵗ du Kassaï
7. Dᵗ de l'Équateur
8. Dᵗ de l'Oubandji et Ouellé
9. Dᵗ de l'Arouwimi et Ouellé
10. Dᵗ des Stanley-Falls
11. Dᵗ du Loualaba

1. Dᵗ Banana
2. Dᵗ Boma
3. Dᵗ Matadi
4. Dᵗ der Watervallen
5. Dᵗ Stanley-Pool
6. Dᵗ Kassaï
7. Evenaarsdistrict
8. Dᵗ Oubandji en Ouellé
9. Dᵗ Arouwimi en Ouellé
10. Stanley-Falls district
11. Dᵗ Loualaba

The offices of the État-Major in Boma, a city situated on the Congo River and the capital of the Congo Free State. (Author's collection)

his command, as well as making sure that military stocks were kept replenished.[27] The FP's headquarters found in Boma, the capital city of the Congo Free State and the Belgian Congo from 1886 to 1923, and from 1891 the artillery and engineering units were based in the Fort de Shinkakasa, some 1.5 kilometres to the west of the city. As for its training camps, these were situated at Nyongo, Bongila, Kasongo, La Romée, Bolobo-Yumbi, Zambi, Umangi, Kasai, Uele, Lokanda, and Ankoro.

In terms of weaponry, the rifle most prominently used by FP foot soldiers was the Albini or Albini-Braendlin rifle. A Belgian version of the Snider-Enfield breach-loading rifle designed by Italian naval officer Augusto Albini and perfected by English gunsmith Francis Braendlin. Single-shot Belgian Terssen Terssen 11 mm rifles were also used in the 1880s with many replaced by the M1870 Belgian Comblain, a falling-block rifle developed by Hubert-Joseph Comblain of Liège. Carbines made by Mauser also saw service as did the Browning pistols used by officers and senior NCOs. Later, the FP used the French-designed Lebel Model 1886 rifle (aka Mle. 1886 M93) that used the bolt action of the Mauser. Albini also produced the cartridges and rounds for the FP's stock of firearms as did Mauser and Browning. The Maxim machine gun also made an appearance in the Congo Free State. One of the most powerful weapons of the time that could fire up to 600 rounds per minute, this recoil-operated machine gun

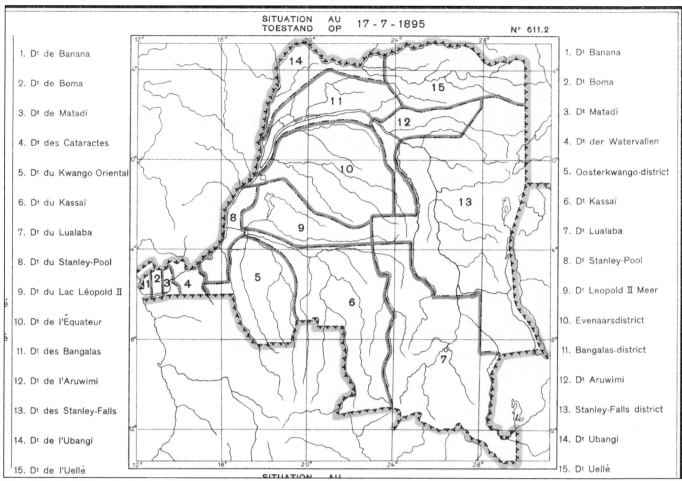

Administrative Divisions in the Congo Free State, 1895. (Institut Royal Colonial Belge)

Force Publique soldiers proudly display the colours of the CFS. (Author's collection)

invented by the American-born British inventor Sir Hiram Stevens Maxim in 1884 has been described as the weapon most associated with imperial conquest and the so-called "Scramble for Africa", the period between the early 1880s and 1914 during which colonial powers divided up the African continent into geographical areas to create new entities.

By 1908, the FP possessed a range of armaments that had been of great service in the campaigns described hereafter. In addition to those described and pictured above, the FP had acquired

Table 4: Belgian Army officers in the armed forces of the International Association of the Congo and the Congo Free State, 1877–1908[22]

Type	Number		Deaths		Total	
	Officers	NCOs	Officers	NCOs	Left the Congo	Died in the Congo
Line regiments	340	771	105	220	1,111	325
Fighting regiments, riflemen, grenadiers	135	311	33	98	446	131
Cavalry	62	209	15	71	271	86
Artillery	65	180	18	55	245	73
Engineering regiments	21	52	6	15	73	21
Backline soldiers	5	20	1	1	2	
Miscellaneous	20	69	4	20	89	29
Total	648	1,612	182	480	2,260	662

Note: 29 percent of all Belgians serving in the Congo died in battle or from illness.

Native recruits received training at several camps around the Congo Free State. (Author's collection)

An inspection of *Force Publique* soldiers at Irebu. (Author's collection)

Table 5: The Commanders-in-chief of the *Force Publique*, 1886–1960					
Name	Rank	Dates	Name	Rank	Dates
Léon Roget	Commandant	August 1886 August 1888	A.C.E. Brunel	Colonel	March 1909 March 1911
Henri Avaert	Commandant	August 1888 October 1889	Auguste Marchant	Lt. Colonel / Colonel	March 1911 January 1916
Léon Van de Putte	Commandant	July 1890 June 1891	Charles Tombeur	Major General	January 1916 May 1918
Léopold Fourdin	Commandant	October 1891 June 1893	Philipe Molitor	Major General	June 1918 April 1920
Georges Dielman	Commandant	June 1893 June 1895	Frederik-Valdemar. Olsen (Danish)	Lt. Colonel / Colonel	October 1920 August 1924
Jules Van Dorpe	Commandant	June 1895 June 1898	Paul-Charles Ermens	Colonel / Major General	November 1925 July 1930
Georges Dielman	Commandant	March 1899 March 1900	Léopold De Konink	Major General	July 1930 July 1932
Ernest Tonglet	Commandant	May 1900 November 1902	Auguste Servais	Colonel	August 1932 November 1933
Gustave Seghers	Commandant	June 1903 December 1903	Emile Hennequin	Colonel / Major General	April 1935 November 1939
Erasme Warnant	Lt-Colonel	May 1904 April 1906	Auguste-Edouard Gilliaert	Lt. Colonel / Colonel	November 1939 December 1940
Joseph Gomins	Colonel	April 1906 May 1907	Paul-Charles Ermens	Lt. General	December 1940 August 1944
Joseph Paternoster	Colonel	May 1907 December 1907	Auguste-Edouard Gilliaert	Major General / Lt. General	August 1944 February 1954
Joseph Gomins	Colonel	March 1908 May 1909	Emile Janssens	Lt. General	February 1954 July 1960

These soldiers wear khaki, the colour of uniform worn after 1917. The uniforms up to that year were navy blue with a red sash around the waist, and red trim around the neck and the front opening. Soldiers also wore a red fez. (Author's collection)

In later years, the *Force Publique* possessed cavalry units. Note the carrying of swords. (Author's collection)

Maxim-Nordenfeldt fortress guns as well as rifle breech loaded cannons manufactured by the Swede Martin von Wahrendorff from 1837. The latter also fitted to boats, 37mm and 75mm cannons made by the German Friedrich Krupp and others produced by French manufacturer Hotchkiss completed a significant arsenal of artillery pieces.

Table 6: Ranks and insignia of the *Force Publique*, 1886–1908

Europeans

Commandant en Chef	Gold braid with 4 gold stripes
Capitaine-Commandant (1re classe)	Gold braid with 3 gold stripes
Capitaine-Commandant (2ème classe)	Gold braid with 2 gold stripes, 1 silver stripe
Capitaine	Gold braid with 2 gold stripes
Lieutenant	Gold braid with 1 gold stripe
Sous-lieutenant	3 gold stripes
Adjudant	2 gold stripes
Sergent major	3 stripes (gold and red wool)
1er Sergent	2 stripes (gold and red wool)
Sergent	1 stripe (gold and red wool)
Agent militaire	2 gold stripes, 2 red stripes
Chef-comptable militaire	2 gold stripes, 1 silver stripe
Premier sous-officier	2 gold stripes, 1 red stripe (wool)
Sous-officier	1 gold stripe, 1 red stripe (wool)
Caporal	3 yellow stripes (wool) worn on both sleeves
Soldat (1re classe)	2 yellow stripes (wool) worn on both sleeves
Soldat (2ème classe)	1 yellow stripe (wool) worn on both sleeves
Adjoint militaire	No insignia

Indigenous Soldiers

Adjudant	4 gold and red stripes (wool)
Sergent major	3 gold and red stripes (wool)
1er Sergent	2 gold and red stripes (wool)
Sergent fourrier	1 gold and red stripe (wool), 1 yellow stripe
Sergent	1 gold and yellow stripe
Caporal	2 yellow stripes
Soldat (1re classe)	1 yellow stripe worn on left sleeve

Note: Stripes were 25 cms long and 2 cms wide. They were placed diagonally at the bottom or on the top half of the sleeve.

Table 7: An inventory of the Force Publique's arsenal of weapons, 1908[28]

Albini rifles with bayonets	25,254
Mauser carbines, rifles	694
Browning pistols	535
Wahrendorff 80 mm cannons	4
Nordenfeldt 57 mm cannons	13
Nordenfeldt 47 mm cannons	62
Nordenfeldt boat cannon	1
Krupp 75 mm cannons (bronze)	24
Krupp 75 mm cannons (steel)	18
Krupp 37 mm cannons (steel)	1
Hotchkiss cannons	2
Maxim machine guns	19
Mortars 21cm	3
Mortars 15cm	3

Note: There were an additional 1,000 rifles used for training purposes (make not specified), as well as 8 other cannons (make not specified), and 24 smooth-bore cannons (make not specified).

Albini cartridges	4,000,000
Albini blank cartridges	1,000,000
Bullet capsules	1,600,000
Mauser cartridges	150,000
Browning cartridges	100,000
Mortar rounds	650
Wahrendorff shells	629
Wahrendorff shells (boat)	308
Krupp shells (75mm, bronze)	4,945
Krupp shells (75mm, steel)	6,152
Krupp shells (37mm, steel)	253
Hotchkiss shells (37mm)	1,902
Nordenfeldt shells (47mm)	14,439
Smooth-bore shells	2,468

Horses were also used to carry machine guns. (Author's collection)

This *Force Publique* officer is pictured wearing a French-model 1886 pattern helmet. (militarysunhelmets.com)

A highly effective weapon firing up to 600 rounds per minute, the FP possessed a Maxim that could be mounted aboard a boat for river borne expeditions. (Author's collection)

A Nordenfeldt is put through its paces while *Force Publique* officers check its range. (Author's collection)

An officer of the *Force Publique* with Askari volunteers. Note blue uniforms. (militarysunhelmets.com)

2
Military Challenges to the Congo Free State

The Congo-Arab War 1892–1894

With the FP growing in strength from 1,487 in 1889 to 10,215 in 1894, 14,779 in 1900, and to 17,833 in 1914,[1] the most prominent military action faced by the Congo Free State occurred when a force led by a certain Tippu Tip attacked a trading station near Stanley Falls. His real name Hamad bin Muhammad bin Juma bin Rajab el Merjebi, Tip had spent most of his life as an explorer, a slave trader and an ivory trader, the proceeds of which he used to set up successful clove plantations in Zanzibar. Over the previous years, Tip had sought to expand his empire taking him to Basoko just north of Stanleyville (Kisangani) and bringing him into contact with both Livingstone and Stanley during his travels. Ivory trading was Tip's specialty, but his settlements around Stanley Falls, Nyangwe, Kasongo and Kabambare enabled him to attack local villages at night and capture sleeping natives who were then sold as slaves and sent along the slave routes to Uvira.

As leader of the Batetela and Bakusu tribes, Tip's slave trading made the situation between Arab and European traders difficult and requiring great diplomacy. Made worse by the fact that the Zanzibaris serving with the *Force Publique* would take Tipp's side in any conflict, in 1884 an agreement was reached that restricted Tipp's slave trading to certain areas. A fragile peace between Arabs and Europeans existing until August 1886, while Tipp travelled to Zanzibar for an extended stay, he was replaced by the much more menacing figure of Bwana N'Zigé. An incident involving his capture of a local woman put the two sides on a war footing, and conflict ensued at the end of the month that resulted in defeat for the Europeans and the realisation that the Arabs could muster much larger forces when needed. A more practical solution to disagreement had to be found, and it was Morton Stanley himself who was given the role of appeasing Tipp's followers. Tipp was subsequently made Vali (governor) of the Stanley Falls district, and up to 1892 both Arabs and Europeans returned to making the most of what the northern areas offered in terms of marketable commodities. Nevertheless, neither side tried to conceal their animosity towards each other, and tensions between the two would soon lead to all-out war. This conflict, the Congo-Arab War of 1892–1894 opposed the FP and those fighting for Tipp's son, Sefu bin Hamid.

Conflict began on 15 March 1892 when Arab forces murdered Lieutenant Hodister, a representative of the Belgian Society of the Upper Congo. Enamoured by this success near Riba Riba, the Arabs then burned down factories belonging to the society and killing everyone working within them. Soon the Arabs were joined by a local chief named Gongo Lutete who had become an ally of Sefu. A member of the Bakassu tribe and another former slave of the Arabs, a detachment of the FP commanded by Lieutenant Francis Dhanis was dispatched to Lusambo to face the threat and regain control of areas lost in a matter of weeks. The first battle between the FP and Lutete's warriors took place on 23 April 1892 while others were fought on 5 and 9 May. The first two indecisive, the third saw Lutete defeated. In the meantime, Sefu had not been inactive and had made his way from Stanley Falls to Kassongo where he had taken Lieutenants Lippens and De Bruyn hostage in the hope they would serve as bargaining chips in future peace negotiations. Their terms refused by the Belgians, Sefu's forces including thousands

Tippu Tip (1832–1905) was an entrepreneur specialising in the trading of ivory and humans. Born in Zanzibar, Tip began trading in ivory and slaves at an early age. (Author's collection)

of Congolese and Swahili warriors marched from Ngangwe and Kassongo and headed for the Lomami River. Dhanis's forces were not as large as his opponent's, it still consisted of seven Europeans, 350 regular troops armed with Snider-Enfields, Winchester rifles (probably the Winchester Model 1890) and a 75mm Krupp field gun. These artillery pieces could fire canister as well as explosive shells.

Aided by a force led by Captain Michaux and several thousand led by the recently defected Lutete, the Battle of Chige started on 23 November 1892 and ended in victory for Dhanis's forces. Determined to defeat the Arabs, Dhanis's forces then took the war into the Arabs' stronghold by launching the Maniema campaign. By that time, his army consisted of some six Belgian officers, 400 regulars and around 16,000 natives, the latter commanded by their own chiefs.[2] Dhanis's campaign was successful despite the conditions faced by his army and the lack of food available due to the ravages of the Arab slave trade. It has been pointed out that Dhanis lost not a single man to sickness or desertion, and that his success can be explained by his allowing his army to travel with their wives, slaves and servants. This enabled soldiers to be burdened only by their weapons and equipment while the wives and slaves carried supplies as Dhanis's caravan moved through Maniema. Another aspect of the campaign was that Dhanis forbade his soldiers to attack villagers not at war, and because these soldiers were accompanied by their wives, they were not generally tempted to molest local women.[3]

Fig. 248.—Large States in the Congo Basin.

Scale 1 : 24,000,000.

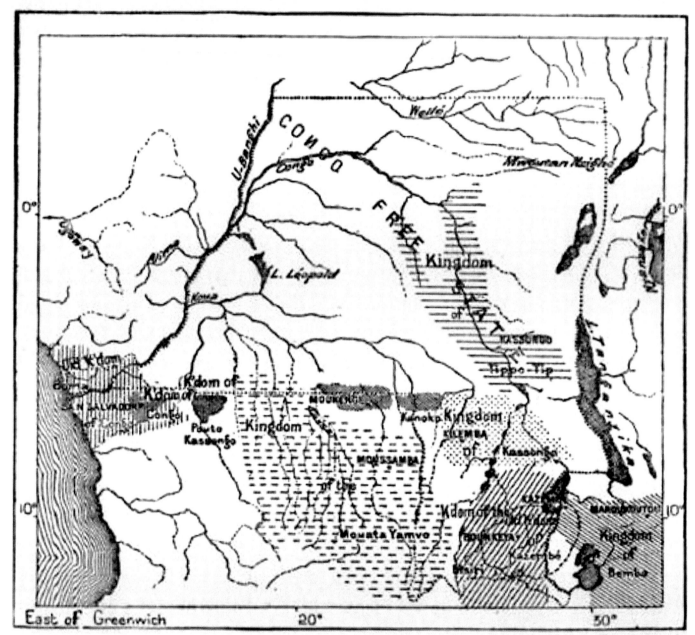

This map shows how the Congo at the end of the 1880s was a blend of different kingdoms. A free-trade zone, the Congo Free State never covered the same land mass as the current day Democratic Republic of the Congo. The area that was controlled by Tippu Tipp can be found on the right of the map. (Author's collection)

The consequence of this was that Dhanis gained the respect of local populations previously mistreated by the Arabs.

The next stage in Dhanis's march to defeat the Arabs was by taking the fight to one of Tippu Tipp's allies, another Tanzanian slave trader called Rumaliza. His real name Muhammad bin Khalfan bin Khamis al-Barwani (born *circa* 1855), in the 1870s and 1880s Rumaliza and Tipp established trading bases in Kasongo in the Congo as well as in Ujiji situated on the eastern bank of Lake Tanganyika. Ujiji would later be used as a stopover point for the transfer of weapons into the Congo from Tanzania during the eastern campaigns of the Congo Crisis (1960–1967), and from here Rumazila organised raids along the Congo's Rusizi River travelling as far as Lake Kivu, a stretch of water lying between the Congo and Rwanda.[4] By 1892, Rumazila had also established slave trading routes that led from Stanley Falls,

travelled along the Lualaba River and traversed Lake Tanganyika to Bagamoyo in Tanzania.

Reinforced by the arrival of Commandant Gillian and Lieutenant Doorme in April 1893, and by Captain Pierre Ponthier and Louis-Napoléon Chaltin in June of that year, Congo Free State forces made short work of Rumazila's army by travelling up the Lomami River to Bena-Kamba, then attacking Riba Riba. The Arab forces also defeated at Stanley Falls in May 1893, then at Kirundu, a settlement controlled by a Comorian named Kiponge, Chaltin went on to defeat the Arabs in the Congo's north-eastern region of Dungu. There was to be one last battle in the Congo-Arab War, and this towards the end of October 1893 on the Luama River to the west of Lake Tanganyika. Making a final stand, Sefu had clashed with a column of Dhanis's troops inflicting over 50 casualties, and this resulted in Dhanis

Fighting at the Arab stronghold of Nyangwe. In Maniema, the town is situated on the Lualaba River and was an important trading point in ivory and slaves for the Arabs. (Author's collection)

Table 8: Loss of *Force Publique* Officers in the Arab Wars, 1892–1895 (All Belgian)[7]				
Name	Rank	Date of death	Place of death	Cause of death
Vrithoff	Ss-officier	05/04/1892	Albertville	KIA
Michiels	Lt.	07/05/1892	Riba Riba	KIA
Lippens	Lt.	01/12/1892	Kasongo	KIA
Debruyne	Ss. Lt.	01/12//1892	Kasongo	KIA
Peters	Ss. Lt.	16/01/1893	Basankusu	KIA
Ponthier	Cdt.	23/10/1893	Mpunga	Died from wounds
De Heusch	Lt.	17/11/1893	Ogella	KIA
Piedboeuf	Capitaine	22/11/1893	Basoko	Sickness
Breugelmans	Ss-officier	05/01/1894	Nyangwe	Sickness
De Woutens	Capitaine	27/04/1894	Kasongo	Sickness
Duvivier	Lt.	07/10/1894	Molino	Accident
Ducoulombier	Ss-officier	15/03/1895	Léopoldville	Sickness
Brexhe	Ss. Lt.	03/04/1895	Kilonga-Longa	Sickness
Stuyvers	Ss-officier	02/05/1895	Avabuki	Sickness
Velghe	Ss. Lt.	24/09/1895	Avabuki	Sickness
Rochet	Lt.	25/12/1895	Kilonga-Longa	Sickness

be a miscarriage of justice and mutinied against their officers at the FP's base in Luluabourg, the current day Kananga. The first mutiny in a long line of revolts targeting FP officers – the last taking place of July 1960 – in July 1895 soldiers of the Tetela tribe murdered several Belgian officers before attacking an FP post at Kabinda. Though numbering fewer than 400, the mutineers moved on to Lusambo and Gandu on the Lomami River, and here they killed more Belgian officers. They were well armed with modern weapons, they had learnt military skills from their service in the FP and, according to one source, were equal to any of the European troops sent to confront them.[8] Furthermore, facing certain execution for having mutinied, the Tetela were ready to fight to the death rather than being captured. A small force under the command of Commandant Lothaire and Lieutenant Gillain was sent to deal with the revolt. It met mutineers near Gandu on 18 October 1895 and following a fierce battle many of the Batetela lay dead while others were captured and taken prisoner. Those that escaped formed into smaller groups and sought refuge in a nearby forest. The cover of the forest provided them with some protection from CFS forces now numbering close to 1,000, the different small groups united a

focusing his attention the Arab leader. Sefu, along with several of his relatives, was killed in the ensuing exchanges between the two sides,[5] as was Kiponge, a man implicated in the killing of the Ottoman naturalist Emin Pasha one year previously. Rumaliza continuing the fight, he was defeated in January 1894 when CFS forces under Captain Hubert Lothaire blew up Rumaliza's ammunition dump as well as his fort, and killed all of its occupants. This signalled the end of the Arab occupation of eastern and north-eastern Congo as Lothaire's troops secured the area and took over 2,000 prisoners.[6]

The Batetela Rebellions and War Against the Madhists

With the Congo-Arab War ending in January 1894 and opening the way for Belgian domination of the Congo, the next threat to the existence of Congo Free State came from within its own boundaries after the execution of Gongo Lutete in 1893. Accused of treason by CFS officials, the soldiers he had brought with him when defecting from Sefu bin Hamid's forces considered Lutete's trial to

few days later and confronted a column of FP soldiers on their way to Maniema. Four Belgian soldiers killed during this confrontation, the next battle between Batetela rebels and the FP took place on 6 November 1895 when forces under Commandant Lothaire launched an attack at Gongo Machoffe. The Batetela suffering heavy losse during this incident and many of those captured handed over to Lothaire by local tribal chiefs, the recent fighting brought this phase of the Batetela Rebellion to an end. However, still bitter about the execution of Lutete and still seeking revenge, a second Batetela mutiny took place as the now Baron Dhanis made his way to the Lado Enclave, a narrow strip of land between lakes Albert and Tanganyika that had become part of the Congo Free State in 1894. Indeed, France was concerned that Léopold held designs on taking over territory controlled by the French north of the Congo, and on the signing of the Franco-Congolese Treaty of 14 August 1894 France accepted Léopold's ownership of the enclave. Not having sufficient resources, it was not until early 1896 that Léopold sent Dhanis to take control

Table 9: Losses in the Madhist Campaign, 1893–1898 (Officers and NCOs)[13]

Name	Rank	Date of death	Place of death	Cause of death
Delmotte	Ss-officier	03/12/1893	Momensi	KIA
Bonvalet	Capitaine	02/03/1894	Bili	KIA
Devos	Ss. Lt.	02/03/1894	Bili	KIA
Ligot	Ss-officier	18/03/1894	Mundu	KIA
Frennet	Ss. Lt.	11/02/1895	Bafuka	KIA
Saroléa	Lt.	17/02/1897	Rejaf	KIA
Cajot	Ss-officier	14/07/1897	Rejaf	Died from wounds
Walhousen	Cdt.	20/05/1898	Rejaf	KIA
Coppejans	Ss. Lt	20/05/1898	Rejaf	KIA
Bienaimé	Ss-officier	20/05/1898	Rejaf	KIA
Desneux	Lt.	04/06/1898	Rejaf	KIA
Bartholi (Italy)	Lt.	04/06/1898	Rejaf	KIA

Table 10: Losses in the Batetela rebellion at Luluabourg 1895 (Officers and NCOs)[14]

Name	Rank	Date of death	Place of death	Cause of death
Pelzer	Capitaine	04/07/1895	Luluabourg	Massacred
Dehaspe	Ss-officier	19/07/1895	Kayeye	Massacred
Bollen	Lt.	05/08/1895	Kayeye	KIA
Nieveler	Ss-officier	05/08/1895	Kabinda	MIA
Augustin	Capitaine	18/08/1895	Ngandu	KIA
Francken	Capitaine	18/05/1895	Ngandu	KIA
Langerbrock	Ss-officier	18/05/1895	Ngandu	KIA
Sandrart	Lt.	13/09/1895	Ngandu	KIA
Decorte	Ss-officier	28/09/1895	Kasongo	Died from wounds
Palate	Ss-officier	08/10/1895	Piane Lombe	KIA
Delava	Lt.	17/10/1895	Piane Lombe	KIA
Collet	Ss. Lt.	17/10/1895	Piane Lombe	KIA
Cassieman	Ss-officier	17/10/1895	Piane Lombe	KIA
Heyse	Ss-officier	17/10/1895	Piane Lombe	KIA
Burke (USA)	Lt.	18/01/1897	Goie-Kabamba	KIA

Note: Lindsay Burke was a 26-year-old from New Orleans. He had been in the Congo less than a year and was killed in an ambush along with 27 of his men.[15] Lindsay Burke was the son of Edward A. Burke, the Democratic State Treasurer of Louisiana.

of the territory. Mounting what is reportedly the largest expedition that nineteenth century Africa had ever seen, Léopold's ambition was to use the Lado Enclave as a means of capturing Khartoum in the Sudan thus opening up a Belgian-controlled passage between the Atlantic and Indian oceans.[9] The enclave having come under attack from Sudanese Mahdists, Commandant Louis-Napoléon Chaltin had driven the Mahdists as far back as the Nile, and was followed by Dhanis whose role was to set up military outposts to ward off further incursions. Dhanis set out with 3,000 men, a third of whom were Batetela tribesmen. In February 1897, a force of 2,000 under the command of Captain Leroi reached Dirfi near Dungu in the Congo, when suddenly the Batetela mutinied killing Leroi and his fellow officers.[10]

Hearing of this, Dhanis turned his attention to putting down the revolt in March 1897. Nonetheless, Dhanis was hampered by around 500 of his Batetela troops switching sides to support their fellow tribesmen and he was forced to retreat. Following this incident in which 10 FP officers lost their lives, the Batetela headed for Stanley Falls destroying trading stations along the way. Finally, it was an outbreak of smallpox among the Batetela that weakened their ability to fight. It was, however, more than a month before sufficient numbers of FP troops could be gathered, and it was not until June 1897 that they encountered the Batetela. The attack on the Batetela camp near Lindi was a resounding success with over 400 Batetela killed with 500 rifles and 10,000 cartridges captured.[11] For the time being, it appeared as though the Batetela revolt was over. There was, nevertheless, to be a final rebellion carried out in 1900 at Fort de Shinkakasa. Though minor when compared to the scale of the revolts of 1895 and 1897, it involved a group of Batetela soldiers taking control of the fort and firing on a Belgian ship docked in the harbour below. Despite the mutiny being rapidly defeated, small groups of Batetela continued to operate against the FP mainly in the Lomami region until Belgium took control of the colony in 1908. Realising that there was the risk of further uprisings inside the FP should one tribe become dominant in number, the army was reorganised accordingly.[12]

At the beginning of the 1890s, both Léopold and British entrepreneurs were keen to secure the rights to mine Katanga's riches, and so the "Scramble for Africa" was epitomised by their respective efforts to lay claim to the south-eastern regions of the Congo. And, though, commercially based disputes between the CFS and the British would eventually be settled through an agreement between Tanganyika Concessions Limited (TCL) and the Société Générale de Belgique (SGB) in order to create the Union Minière du Haut-Katanga (UMHK) in 1906, to obtain mining rights in the province in 1891 both sides faced a formidable hurdle in the shape of yet another Arab slave trader named Mwenda Msiri Ngelengwa Shitambi, or more commonly Msiri. Referred to as M'Siri by the Belgians, over the previous decades this native of Tabora in Tanzania had followed in the footsteps of his father, Kalassa, and Tippu Tip by taking ivory and slaves from the interior of Africa and taking what were considered as commodities along a trading route that passed through Ujiji and continued to Zanzibar. From this archipelago

Table 11: Losses (Officers and NCOs) during Dhanis's Expedition, 1896–1898[16]				
Name	Rank	Date of death	Place of death	Cause of death
Docquier	Lt.	23/11/1896	Irumu	Sickness
Van Lint	Lt.	25/12/1896	Irumu	Sickness
Mathieu	Cdt.	03/01/1897	Andemobe	Suicide
Tagon	Ss-officier	14/02/1897	Mongwa	Massacred
Andrianne	Ss-officier	14/02/1897	Mongwa	Massacred
Von Melen (Swede)	Ss-officier	15/02/1897	Mongwa	Massacred
Inver (Turk)	s / Intendant	15/02/1897	Mongwa	Massacred
Leroy	Cdt.	15/02/1897	Mongwa	Massacred
Closet	Ss-officier	19/02/1897	Mongwa	KIA
Julien	Cdt.	18/03/1897	Ekwanga	KIA
Cronenborg (Swede)	Capitaine	18/03/1997	Ekwanga	KIA
De La Court	Lt.	18/03/1997	Ekwanga	KIA
Crahay	Ss-officier	19/03/1897	Irumu	Massacred
Dhanis Louis	Intendant	24/03/1897	Ikuru	KIA
De Bus	Ss-officier	10/05/1897	La Romée	Sickness
Hambursin	Cdt.	14/05/1897	Stanleyville	Sickness
Dubois Evrard	Lt.	13/11/1897	Birizi	KIA
Melaerts	Lt.	23/12/1897	Boko	KIA
Langhans	Cdt.	03/01/1898	Simorane	KIA
De Connick	Ss-officier	08/02/1898	Bakare	Sickness
Eliard	Ss officier	14/02/1898	Lukili	Sickness
Bricourt	Ss-officier	22/03/1898	Mbelia	Sickness
Debergh	Cdt.	18/05/1898	Ngabo	KIA
Donckier	Lt.	26/07/1898	Andmobe	Friendly fire
Lardy (Swiss)	Capitaine	04/11/1898	Sungula	KIA
Ardevel	Ss-officier	04/11/1898	Sungula	KIA
Swensson (Swede)	Cdt.	13/11/1898	Kabambare	Sickness
Sterckx	Lt.	14/11/1898	Kabambare	KIA
Rahbeck (Dane)	Lt.	14/11/1898	Kabambare	KIA

Note: An intendant performed administrative duties. s / Intendant is an abbreviation of sous-intendant (second intendant).

warriors were used by Msiri to conquer lands inhabited by the Luba. The wars between the two tribes a continuation of a rivalry that dated back to the fifteenth century, the legacy of this ancient rivalry continued up to the early 1960s and, along with the financial considerations of Katanga's secession, played a role in Tshombe's decision to form a breakaway state in July 1960.

Now controlling a vast swathe of the Congo, Msiri knew that others would come looking for his mineral riches, but in the 1870s, Katanga belonged to him. At the head of a quasi-monopoly over trade in Katanga, he set about building an army capable of defending the province by trading salt, slaves, iron and copper for arms and ammunition. He traded these wares with the Arabs of East Africa, with Rhodesian, Tanganyikan, Ugandan, and Angolan tribes as well as the Portuguese, and after making Bunkeya in the Congo the centre of his operations he warded off enemies by hanging severed heads around his encampment and buying more slaves to serve in his army.[17] Decapitation and cannibalism were familiar practices in attempts to dissuade enemy attacks in the Congo.[18] Other methods used by Msiri to command respect were throwing women into pits containing starving dogs, and cutting out of his wives' hearts while they were still alive and sucking the blood out of them. Men were also tied to trees to starve, and when they complained they were fed their own ears, noses and arms so that they devoured themselves alive.[19] At the height of his power, Msiri – now chief of the Bayeke tribe – kept a harem of some 600 wives and commanded an army of some 10,000 men of whom 3,000 were armed with rifles.[20] This was the state of affairs when European explorers such as Stanley first began to make inroads into Africa's interior. Msiri's Bayeke tribe dominated Katanga, and this was what Léopold's *Force Publique* was to come up against around the same time that Lothaire confronted Sefu bin Hamid's forces further north.

Msiri's belief that others would come after Katanga's riches came true in 1890 when Cecil Rhodes sent Alfred Sharpe and Joseph Thomson to Bunyeka to act as his emissaries and obtain rights to mine areas under Msiri's control. Thomson was blocked *en route* by an outbreak of smallpox, and Sharpe's mission also failed once Msiri understood the intentions of the treaties.[21] Notwithstanding these failures, Léopold was aware that Rhodes would make further

situated off the coast of Tanzania, hundreds of thousands of slaves as well as ivory and cloves were dispatched to the Middle East via the Indian Ocean. As for Msiri, he became so successful that by 1856 he had managed to secure around half a million square kilometres of the Congo for himself and had become the ruler of the Bayeke (or Garanganze) Kingdom that stretched from the Luvua River in the north to the Congo-Zambezi in the south, and from Lake Mweru and the Luapala River in the east to the Lualaba River in the west. Northwards lay lands controlled by Tippu Tip. (See Map 2)

The creation and growth of the Bayeke Kingdom took place after Kalassa had been presented with copper ingots purchased by a party of Bayeke hunters. Realising that this yellow-coloured metal was valuable, he was eager to add it to his list of tradable commodities and so befriended Chief Katanga, the man after whom the province is named. The friendship was sealed with Msiri marrying one of the chief's daughters and was betrayed when Msiri poisoned his father-in-law and subsequently waged war against his wife's brother. Next, Msiri befriended members of the Lunda tribe in Katanga and Lunda

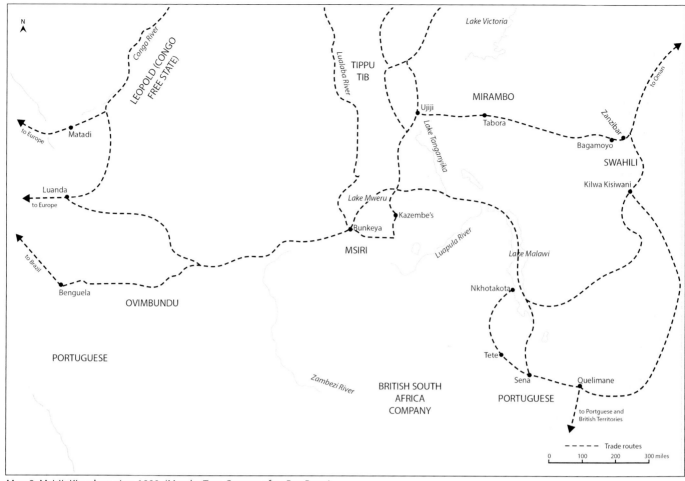

Map 2. Msiri's Kingdom *circa* 1880. (Map by Tom Cooper, after Rex Parry)

attempts to negotiate with Msiri. A major obstacle when it came to organising his own expeditions, however, was that Léopold lacked the finances to initiate any consequential move to annex Katanga. Indeed, projects to increase the size of the Congo Free State's

Captain William Grant Stairs was born in Halifax, Nova Scotia on 1 July 1863. An officer in the *Force Publique*, Stairs died from malaria on 9 June 1892. (Author's collection)

Captain Omer Bodson, the *Force Publique* officer who shot and killed Msiri on 20 December 1891. (Demetrius C. Boulger, *The Congo State: Or, the growth of civilisation in Central Africa*, 1898)

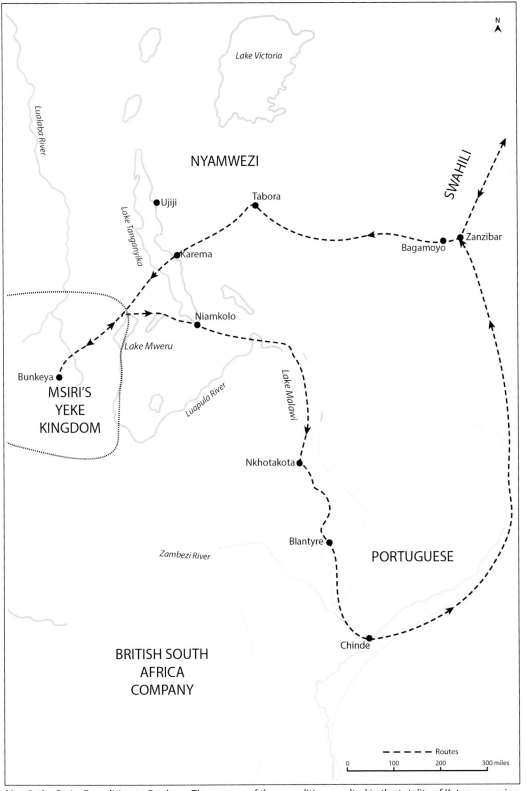

Map 3: the Stairs Expedition to Bunkeya. The success of the expedition resulted in the totality of Katanga coming under Belgian control and an end to the slave trade in the Congo. (Map by Tom Cooper, after Rex Parry)

than four separate expeditions to Katanga, the first of which was led by Paul Le Marinel.

As was common policy in colonial attempts to annex parts of Africa, Le Marinel offered Msiri Léopold's protection from attack by his enemies. The suggestion dismissed out of hand, and Le Marinel ordered to leave the area, fellow FP officer Alexandre Delcommune led an expedition along the Lomami River into Katanga, headed east to the Lualaba River and crossed the Hakansson Mountains to arrive in the Lufira Valley. Arriving in Bunkeya on 6 October 1891, Delcommune's efforts also failed and he, too, was ordered to leave Katanga. Though Msiri was angered by Léopold's attempts, negotiations led to the Bayeke chief inviting Rhodes to claim Katanga for Great Britain, yet another Belgian-led expedition was already under way, and this time it had been financed by the CK.[22] Led by Captain William Stairs, a Nova Scotia-born British officer serving in the *Force Publique*, it followed an 1886 expedition involving Stairs which consisted of relieving Emin Pasha, Charles Gordon's the governor of Equitoria, an area of South Sudan threatened by Madhist forces. Known as the Emin Pasha Relief Expedition and led by Henry Morton Stanley, Stairs had acted as the expedition's second-in-command. As regards to the Katanga expedition, Stair's second-in-command was the only Belgian on the route to meet Msiri. Named Captain Omer Bodson, this FP officer gained notoriety when he shot

network of railways were proving to be more costly than expected, rubber quotas were not being met – hence the brutal methods used to increase production – and, from a military point of view, as we have seen, Léopold's armed forces were wrapped up in expensive expeditions near the border with Sudan. Some form of financial assistance was obtained, nonetheless, in the shape of an agreement struck with the SGB. This allowed for the creation of the *Compagnie du Congo pour le Commerce et l'Industrie* (CCCI) and the *Compagnie de Katanga* (CK), and between 1891 and 1893 Léopold sent no fewer

and killed Msiri on 20 December 1891 leaving the way open for Léopold to claim the whole of Katanga for the Congo Free State. The Stairs Expedition, as it has become known, used 400 Africans including around 100 Askaris and "pagazis" or porters. Mostly Zanzibaris hired in Mombasa or Tabora – two towns on the route to Bunkeya – eight Askari from Dahomey (located within modern-day Benin) had also been recruited to serve as riflemen. The presence of these African mercenaries somewhat dispelling the myth that the Scramble for Africa was entirely a European affair involving Europeans only, the annexing of Katanga played a major role in

Table 12: Loss of *Force Publique* Officers in Katanga, 1891–1900[23]

Name	Rank	Date of death	Place of death	Cause of death
Hakansson (Swe.)	Capitaine	30/08/1891	Kibondja	KIA
Bodson	Capitaine	20/12/1891	Majembe	KIA
Stairs (GB)	Capitaine	08/06/1892	Chinde	Sickness
Bia	Capitaine	30/08/1892	Tenke	Sickness
Brasseur	Cdt.	08/11/1897	Chiwala	KIA
De Windt	Geologist	09/08/1898	Lake Tanga	Accident
Catsley	Assistant	09/08/1898	Lake Tanga	Accident
Fromont	Ss-Lt.	20/03/1899	Mulumba	KIA

British missionaries stand alongside men holding hands severed by ABIR militiamen. (rarehistoricalphotos.com)

Sentries employed by the Anglo-Indian Rubber Company. These militia were responsible for enforcing harsh punishments meted out to increase the production of rubber and to meet quotas. Note that the flag of the CFS is depicted on the clothing of the sentry on the right of this photo. (Author's collection)

the elimination of Arab slave trading that had blighted the Congo for many centuries.

Whereas the British did eventually succeed in obtaining a share in Katanga's riches through the creation of the UMHK, and this enabling the exploitation of the richest deposits of copper in the world in terms of their size and value per ton of mineral extracted,[24] horrific events taking place in Congo Free State in regards to native populations were soon to become public knowledge putting increasing pressure on Léopold II, a king who had never set foot in a land over which his agents exercised a brutal authority in order to increase commercial output. Effectively, in addition to the mainly Belgian immigration that took part at the turn of the century, the sheer size of the Free State meant that the concessionary companies to which Léopold had sold trading rights relied heavily on the use of local labour to fully exploit the produce his possession had to offer. The terrain of the Congo varying greatly from region to region, the difficulties linked to the transportation of goods over long distances were overcome by the sometimes-forced recruitment of the Congolese as carriers or porters. So significant was the amount of goods transported out of the inner reaches of the Congo to its ports that from 1892 to 1898 the number of carriers increased from 40,000 to 2,730,533.[25] Starting in 1890, the harvesting of rubber was the industry in which most cutters and porters were used. Obtained from a species vine named the *Landolphia*, rubber was a highly profitable commodity from which ventures such as the Anglo-Belgian India Rubber Company (ABIR) could make enormous profits. In one year, ABIR made a turnover of 100 percent of its initial stake,[26] with Léopold earning a profit of some 70

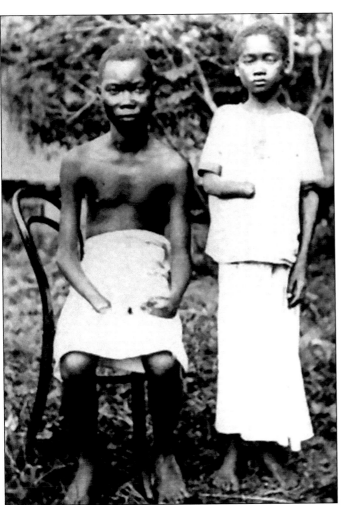

The mutilation of children was a method frequently used to encourage Congolese labourers to increase the harvest of rubber. (Gettyimages)

million Belgian francs purely through the exploitation of rubber.[27] Ivory was another profitable commodity for concessions such as the *Compagnie Anversoise du Commerce au Congo* (CACC) and it was estimated that ivory valued at three and a half million francs was sold in Antwerp in the two years after the company was founded.[28]

It was the reports of the treatment of the Congolese carriers and the Congolese population at large by Léopold's agents that was to lead to the Congo Free State being wound up as an entity and the Belgian government taking control of the Congo. These reports told of atrocities having been committed against native groups residing in the Congo Basin, and they sparked the intervention of the Aborigines Protection Society (APS) of Great Britain which subsequently pressured the British government into launching an enquiry into conditions for the Congolese under Léopold in 1903. It then published Henry Richard Fox Bourne's *Civilisation in Congoland, a Story of International Wrong-Doing* the same year,[29] and this work told of how tribal chiefs would be held prisoner until their people harvested the required amount of rubber, how women and children were beaten with the *chicotte* (a whip made from animal hide); and how villages were burned to the ground when quotas were not met.[30] One of the most notorious punishments sometimes meted out by soldiers of the FP itself, was the severing of hands and feet of villagers employed to harvest rubber. Oftentimes, this punishment was carried out by private militias employed by companies such as ABIR. Other abuses of the Congolese population involved the construction of the railway that linked Matadi and Stanley Pool from 1890 to 1897. Of the thousands recruited by force, the rate of mortality for labourers working on the line reached 8.8 percent in 1892.[31]

As the reports filtered out, in 1903 the British government reacted by sending its Vice-Consul in the Congo, Roger Casement, to inspect conditions. His damning report published one year later, and further reports by British journalist Edmund Dene Morel in the same year led to the setting up of the Commission of Reforms to examine the role of Léopold's agents. Reform decrees were issued and at the end of 1907 and Léopold found himself obliged by the Belgian government to surrender his possessions in central Africa. Through the ratification of the Colonial Charter, the Congo Free State became the Belgian Congo on 15 November 1908.

3
The *Force Publique*, 1908–1918

For the FP, the transfer of power from Léopold to the Belgian government did not lead to any major changes as regards the purpose of the Congo's military forces, or concerning their organisational structure. In fact, the Congo's new authorities chose to pursue a policy whereby the FP served as a means of preserving order throughout the entirety of the territory annexed in November 1908. Effectively, the number of companies reflected the number of administrative districts, the role of Commander-in-chief of the FP remained unchanged as did the Commander-in-chief himself (Colonel Joseph Gomins), and the Commander-in-chief still answered to a Governor General of the colony, himself a serving officer of the FP as were the commissioners of each of the 21 districts. As an illustration of how little administrative attitudes to colonial rule were to change in the immediate years following the annexation of the CFS, the first Governor General of the Belgian Congo was Lieutenant General Théophile Wahis had also served as Governor General of the CFS from 1892–1896 and from 1900–1908. Remaining in office until 23 December 1915, Wahis oversaw the

Belgian Congo's initial participation in the Great War, a subject to which we shall return hereafter.

The FP more or less a territorial police force responsible for preserving order within the limits of the Belgian Congo, its role, its organisational structure and its size would not have enabled authorities to withstand any major uprising notwithstanding the weaponry inherited from the CFS, the firepower of eight 160mm guns of the *Compagnie d'Artillerie et de Génie* based at Boma, and the integration into the FP of the *Troupes de Katanga* in 1910.[1] These guns among the largest ever mounted in Africa, despite certain structural frailties the FP was able to respond to a serious incident that arose in July 1909. In effect, the "Kivu frontier incident" saw the FP dispatched to Mount Ufumbiro (aka the Virunga Mountains) to confront British then German forces. The British forces acting on the authority of John Methuen Coote, Great Britain attempted to claim the territory citing agreements drawn up with Germany in 1894. A subsequent agreement made on 19 May 1909 saw Germany cede any claim to Ufumbiro in exchange for it retaining areas around the

Boma - Départ du Comte de Turin
S. A. R. passant devant le front des troupes

Prince Albert visits the Belgian Congo in 1909. Pictured at Boma, he became Albert I of Belgium on 23 December of that year. (Open source)

Boma - Départ de S. A. R. le Prince Albert - Troupe présentant les armes

Soldiers of the *Force Publique* present arms to HRH the Count of Turin during Albert's visit. (Open source)

numbered 2,875.[3] The Belgian Congo, now divided into four provinces (Congo-Kasai, Equateur, Orientale Province and Katanga) by virtue of a royal order of 28 July 1914, the FP itself was staffed by four main provincial battalions plus two other infantry battalions, a cyclist company, and a headquarters. Of the 17,500, 450 were European officers or NCOs. As per 1914, the FP's arsenal remained essentially the same as in 1908 (see Table 7). White officers and NCOs were issued with M1889 Mauser rifles and Browning pistols while the Congolese Askari carried single-shot 11 mm Albini rifles. As for the *Troupes de Katanga*, they were better armed carrying M1889 Mausers and Masden Light machine guns.[4]

As was the case in Europe, Belgian forces in the Congo had hoped that they would not be drawn into the First World War even if they were informed on 30 July to expect it. The First World War in sub-Saharan Africa fought in four main geographical zones (east, west, north and south), any hope that Belgium could stay out of the war came to an end on the night of 14/15 August after German East Africa (GEA) mobilised its colonial army, the *Schutztrupp*. With the intent of expanding areas under German control, German steamers operating on Lake Tanganyika

Kilimanjaro massif. The agreements serving as a means of defining borders between German East Africa and the British colony of Uganda, FP troops led by Commandant Frederik-Valdemar Olsen were rushed to the area to stop territory belonging to the Belgian Congo from being divided up by two foreign powers.

The presence of Olsen's troops resulting in a 10-month standoff by virtue of these territorial disputes, Britain and Belgium signed the Uganda-Congo Boundary Convention on 14 May 1910 while Britain and Germany signed another agreement in August of that year. Culminating in the Anglo-German-Belgian Commission of 1911,[2] further conflict over which colonial power controlled which swaths of East Africa was avoided for another three years.

In the years that separated the Kivu frontier incident and the outbreak of the First World War, the FP saw a series of organisational changes that led to total military forces in the Congo comprising some 17,500 men. The non-Katangan districts had 12,133 men, those in training amounted to 2,400, and the *Troupes de Katanga*

bombarded the port of Mokolubu on 15 August and attacked an FP post at Lukaga on 22 August. One of these steamers, the *Hedwig von Wissmann,* disabled the Belgian steamer *Alexandre Delcommune.* In view of these attacks, on 28 August 1914 the Belgian government authorised the Vice-Governor of Katanga, Charles Tombeur, to take all measures to defend Belgian territory. This effectively ending Belgian neutrality, Tombeur was given the authority to allow British troops into Katanga to assist in defending the Congo, and to allow Belgian troops to cooperate with British troops in Northern Rhodesia, another area that had come under attack from German forces. Similarly, the Belgian government authorised Congolese forces to reinforce French and British troops in the invasion of the German colony of Kamerun (now Cameroon), a colony lying on the west coast of Africa and to the north of the Belgian Congo.

These members of the *Compagnie de cyclistes* are shown at Baudouinville (now Kirungu) in 1916. Paradoxically, mercenary commander 'Bob' Denard would use this means of transport to invade the Congo in January 1968. (MRA)

12. Cyclistes de la Force Publique
Fietsers der Landmacht

This photo illustrates how officers were also required to ride bicycles. In the Belgian Congo, the Cyclist Company of the *Force Publique* was based in Katanga. (Open source)

the FP, it fitted into plans to land a force at Victoria (now Limbe) on the south-west coast of Kamerun. The French attacking from bases situated in Chad and capturing Kousséri in the north, with the aid of cruisers HMS *Challenger* and HMS *Cumberland*, the Kamerun capital Douala was captured through a Franco-*Force Publique* military collaboration on 27 September 1914. The same force then followed the German-built railway inland, and by November 1914 it had captured Juande (now Yaounde). German forces retreating westwards to the Spanish colony of Rio Muni (now Equatorial Guinea) or to the mountainous interior of Kamerun, by December 1915 the joint forces of French and FP troops had occupied Neukamerun in the west of Kamerun forcing German commander Carl Heinrich Zimmerman to conclude that the war in this part of Africa was lost. The contingent of FP troops returning to Boma on 1 April 1916, the result of the Allied victory was that Great Britain and France divided up Kamerun with the partition accepted at the Paris Peace Conference 1919–1920.

The FP garrisons between Lake Edward (on the border between the DRC and Uganda) and the northern end of Lake Tanganyika distributed as follows: Ruchuru – 360, Bobandana – 190, Kwijwi – 50, Nya Lukemba – 325, Uvira – 375 giving a total of 1,300

The *Force Publique* in the Kamerun Campaign and the East Africa Campaign

The military campaigns of the FP focused on the German colony of Kamerun (modern-day Cameroon), German East Africa, and Northern Rhodesia, the initial role of the 600 FP troops in Kamerun consisted of supporting French and British invasion forces who had entered the country from French Equatorial Guinea on 6 August 1914 and those crossing the border from Nigeria on 25 August. The French under General Joseph Gaudérique Aymerich meeting little resistance in the east of Kamerun, the first engagement between the British West Africa Frontier Force (WAFF) and the *Schutztrupp* occurred during the Battle of Tepe. After moving eastwards, the FP subsequently defeated German forces at the Battle of Nsanakong on 30 August and the First Battle of Garua from 29–31 August. As for

troops,[5] German forces once again targeted control of the Congo's maritime borders when on 24 September 1914 they successfully raided the small post on the island of Kwijwi on Lake Kivu capturing the Belgian detachment.[6] No other major incidents were reported in this area over the following days, but on 4 October a Belgian operation launched from Ruchuru failed in its attempt to dislodge German forces at Kisenyi. In the Kigezi district, a 75-strong Belgian force was also sent to reinforce Ugandan Police posts. Nonetheless, neither side seemed to be seeking to launch any major offensive, and by the end of October 1914, the situation in the northern areas of the Congo remained pretty much as it was when war broke out some three months previously. This stalemate was assured by the arrival of the Indian Expeditionary Force (IEF) to support the British King's African Rifles (KAR), and the Ugandan Police, and

Table 13: The Make-up of the *Force Publique* at the outbreak of the First World War	
Congo-Kasai Province	Léopoldville (capital)
Bas-Congo Company	Kinshasha
Moyen-Congo Company	Léopoldville
Kwango Company	Bandundu
Kasai Company	Luebo
Sankuru Company	Lusambo
Equateur Province	Coquihatville (capital)
Equateur Company	(Coquihatville)
Lake Léopold II Company	(Inongo)
Lulonga Company	(Basankusu)
Bangala Company	(Lisala)
Ubangi Company	(Libenge)
Orientale Province	Stanleyville (capital)
Haut-Uele Company	(Buta)
Bas-Uele Company	(Niangara)
Aruwimi Company	(Basoko)
Stanleyville Company	(Stanleyville)
Lowa Company	(Ponthienville)
Maniema Company	(Kasongo)
Ituri Company	(Irumu)
Kivu Company	(Rutshura)
Katanga Province	Elisabethville (capital)
Tanganika-Moero Company	(Kongolo)
Haut-Luapula Company	(Kambove)
Lulua Company	(Kafakumba)
Lomami Company	(Kabinda)
Cyclist Company	
Training academy for black NCOs	(Elisabethville)
Training bases	
Lukula Bavu	(Mayumbe)
Moamba	(Kasai)
Irebu	(Equateur)
Lisala	(Bangala)
La Tota	(Uele)
Artillery Company	
Shinkakasa Fort	(Boma)
Territorial Police	
One brigade or company in each district, and an additional brigade in Haut-Luapula	

Force Publique soldiers were deployed to Kamerun in August 1914 to assist French forces. (Kaisergrübercollection – Sonck)

The battles fought by French, British, and Belgian troops were fought to stop the spread of the German Empire in West Africa. (Kaisergrübercollection – Sonck)

clothing to last for a year.[7] The battle also described as one of the most notable failures in British military history and leading to 360 soldiers under British command killed, the Battle of Tanga coincided with the Battle of Kilimanjaro (3 November 1914). The German defence of Tanga also coincided with an effort by von Lettow to nullify British forces on Lake Tanganyika and in Northern Rhodesia. As for British naval presence on Lake Tanganyika, it was eliminated with the capturing and sinking of the lake steamer *Cecil Rhodes* on 18/19 November 1914, and to neutralise British forces in Northern Rhodesia, German forces had begun incursions into the British colony in September. Here, German moves to obtain the gradual domination of the southernmost areas of Lake Tanganyika began when on 5 September *Schutztruppe* attacked a garrison of the Northern Rhodesian Police (NRP) at Abercorn (now Mbala). A key outpost for British colonial forces, although the first attack was repulsed and the garrison reinforced by the arrival of a NRP Mobile Column based in Livingstone, the British District Commissioner at Kawambwa decided to request reinforcements and called on FP troops in respect to the agreements made after German attacks on Belgian positions in August 1914. At the time when Abercorn came under attack, the FP's 2nd Battalion headquartered at Albertville was guarding the western shore of Lake Tanganyika and had a detachment at Baudouinville (now Kirungu). The 1st Battalion under Lieutenant Leleux was assembled at Kitope, and the 3rd Battalion under Major Frederick Olsen was prepared for battle at Pweto near Lake Mweru, a body of water situated in Katanga and west of Abercorn. Armed with Mauser rifles, some of the Belgian troops were members of cyclist companies.[8]

Travelling through Mporokoso situated some 75km to the southeast of Lake Mweru, Lelux arrived in Abercorn on 22 September.

the presence of these military forces dissuaded German commander Emil von Lettow-Vorbeck from implementing plans to invade Uganda. Much was to change in East Africa, however, during the Battle of Tanga (3–5 November 1914) when the IEF attacked this Tanzanian port. Also known as the Battle of the Bees, eventual victory by German forces and the retreat of British forces resulted in the *Schutztruppe* acquiring modern rifles, 600,000 rounds of ammunition, Maxim machine guns, field telephones, and enough

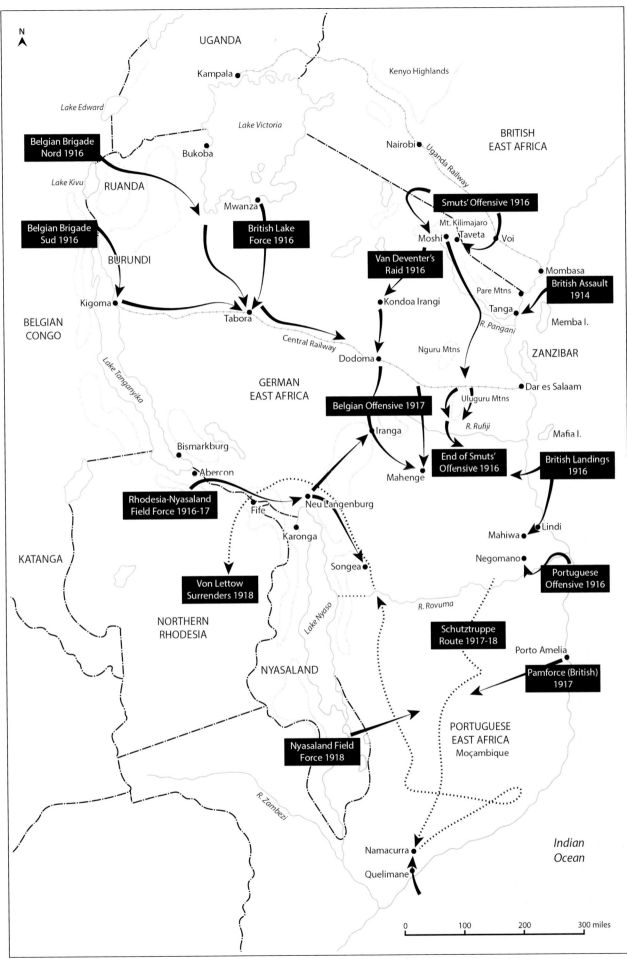

Map 5: The East African Campaign, 3 August 1914 – 25 November 1918. (Map by Tom Cooper)

The fort at Abercorn. An outpost of the Northern Rhodesian Police, the fort was attacked by German forces in early September 1914. The attack brought the *Force Publique* into Northern Rhodesia. (Author's collection)

Force Publique cycle units make their way to provide support for the Northern Rhodesia Police. (Author's collection)

Major Frederick Olsen, one of the most experienced officers in the *Force Publique* and the commander of its 3rd Battalion based in Katanga. (Author's collection)

Followed by Olsen who arrived on 25 September, as with earlier encounters with German forces further north, nothing significant took place and, in November, it was decided that the *Force Publique* troops should return to the Congo. This was in spite of raids carried out between 17–19 November when German forces landed by craft operating on Lake Tanganyika attacked the villages of Kituta and Kasakalawe. These raids were stopped by a 150-strong force under Olsen that was sent to the area.[9]

In a situation that contrasted strikingly with events taking place in Europe in the first six months of 1915, during the next eight months or so the activities of the NRP-FP coalition in Northern Rhodesia were principally limited to patrolling border areas lest further German incursions were made along the coast. This said, and the enemy having increased in size and showing signs that it was ready to launch a major offensive, in December 1914 the decision was made to create an additional post some 30 miles east of Abercorn, and in an area where GEA forces might be offered a point of entry that was undefended. The new fortress set up at Saisi, it was garrisoned by 400 soldiers of the coalition and commanded by Lieutenant-Colonel F.A. Hodson of the NRP. Serving alongside him were six British officers and six officers of the Force Publique's 1st Battalion. The armaments present at the fort included machine guns and a 47mm Nordenfelt.[10]

By June 1915 it had become apparent that Germany was preparing to attack Saisi, and on the 28th of that month GEA forces attempted to surround the fort having approached it using the network of waterways leading off the River Saisi. Once again, the attack was repulsed, and with Hodson replaced by Major O'Sullevan, on 25 July a larger German force comprising some 800 men made a renewed attempt to capture the fort. The attack was made using shelling from two German guns, but no attempt was made by the infantry to overwhelm the manned trenches that surrounded the fort. Conversely, the rifles used by the forces inside the fort did not have the range to reach enemy positions. GEA forces dug in some 600–1,400 yards (548–1,280m) away, this was beyond the capacity of the .303 Martini-Enfield, or .450 Martini-Henry issued to riflemen. On the 28 July 1915, the garrison at Saisi was reinforced by 350 men of the 1st Battalion who had made their way from Abercorn, and with the arrival of these forces GEA commanders became convinced that the only outcome of the battle would be another stalemate. Despite issuing demands for a surrender, GEA forces decided to withdraw from the area on 3 August.

Though the confrontation at Saisi was almost insignificant in comparison to contemporary battles in Belgium – the Second Battle of Ypres resulting in over 59,000 British casualties – it almost ensured that no further German incursions were made into Northern Rhodesia for the remainder of the First World War. Instead, Belgian efforts were switched so that the focus of their attention was areas further north. In the meantime, however, there remained the question of who controlled Lake Tanganyika.

The Battle for Lake Tanganyika

As the number of GEA troops available to von Lettow increased from early 1915, so did the fears that German control of Lake Tanganyika would result in an invasion of the Belgian Congo from the east. This was problematic, as at that time neither Belgium nor Great Britain possessed sufficient numbers of troops to launch an offensive to ward off a large-scale German attack. Indeed, while the Belgians could muster enough forces to carry out attacks in areas bordering the northern part of GEA, this left hundreds of miles of lake coastline open. The only option then, was to regain control of Lake Tanganyika thus nullifying the threat posed by the GEA in this area. To make matters worse for the Belgian-British allied forces, by February 1915 the Germans were preparing to introduce a more powerful warship into Lake Tanganyika from the fortified port of Kigoma in Tanzania. Named the *Graf von Götzen*, this auxiliary warship weighed 1,200 tons, could carry 800 troops, and was mounted with weapons including a 105mm (4-inch) cannon and two 37mm Hotchkiss revolver guns.

With the Germans already having two steamers under military orders – the 60-ton *Hedwig von Wissmann* and the 45-ton *Kingani* – efforts to counter the threat on Lake Tanganyika consisted once again of a Belgian-British naval cooperation that began as early as March 1915. On the Belgian side, in that month it was decided that a new command unit dealing purely with Lake Tanganyika would be set up, and command of this unit was firstly given to Major Stinglhamber then to Lieutenant-Colonel

Georges Moulaert. The troops making up the naval force were from the FP's naval force based at Albertville and those from the 6th FP Battalion under the command of Commandant Borgerghoff.[11] The first job of this unit was to construct an 80-metre jetty that would be long enough for the naval force's fleet of vessels, plus the construction of a dry dock in which a new craft, the *Baron Dhanis*, could be assembled. To offer protection for the port at Albertville, Belgium sent two Krupp 75mm cannons, while two batteries of 160mm cannons were transported from the fort at Shinkakasa. Concurrently, in April 1915, a veteran of the Second Boer War named John Lee proposed that a naval detachment operating light motorboats be formed to counter the threat on Lake Tanganyika. The Belgians supporting this idea, it was subsequently ratified by Sir Henry Jackson of the British Admiralty, and the Royal Navy's Lieutenant-Commander Geoffrey Spicer-Simson was appointed to

EST AFRICAIN ALLEMAND (Occupation Belge)   Le S.S. "Götzen"
DUITSCH OOST AFRIKA (Belgische Bezetting)   De Stoomboot "Götzen"

The SS *Götzen* was constructed at the Meyer shipyard in Papenburg, Germany at a cost of £20,000. Once completed, it was dismantled, packed into 5,000 crates and shipped to Dar es Salaam. From here, the crates were transported across German East Africa on the Central Railway to Kigoma. (Open source)

The crew of the *Graf von Götzen* loading an SK L/40 *Schnelladekanone* (quick-firing gun) retrieved from the SMS *Königsberg*, a cruiser scuttled after the Battle of the Rufiji Delta (October 1914 – July 1915). (Open source)

The two 160mm cannons sent to Albertville had previously been used to protect the mouth of the River Congo. (Author's collection)

HMS *Mimi* and HMS *Toutou* embarked on an epic voyage from London to Lake Tanganyika in June 1915. Here, one of the craft is made ready for transportation by rail from Cape Town. (Open source)

The *Alexandre Delcommune*. Sunk by German forces in 1915, it was re-floated in 1916 and rebaptised *"Le Vengeur"*, or *"The Avenger"*. (Panorama du Congo Belge)

to Bukama in the Lomami province. Then floated down the Lualaba River and across Lake Kisale, they arrived at Kabalo on 22 October. Here, Spicer-Simson met up with FP Commandant Stinghlamber and naval commander, Commandant Goor.[12]

While the Germans had strengthened the firing capacity of the *Götzen* with the retrieval of an SK L/40 *Schnelladekanone* from the cruiser SMS *Köningsberg*, the Belgians had also made slight improvements to its fleet of naval craft, firstly by repairing the *Alexandre Delcommune* (renamed *Le Vengeur* or the 'avenger') and, secondly, by fitting a whaling-boat with an outboard motor and weaponry.

Named the *Netta*, a 37mm cannon was fitted mid-ship. Despite it also being designated as a torpedo boat, no torpedo could be found to suit the vessel. Another advantage was that the *Force Publique* had begun to deploy several seaplanes to act as spotters. The deployment of seaplanes began on 21 November 1915 when Captain-Commander de Bueger was appointed to put together an air unit capable of providing naval surveillance. De Bueger recruited three pilots from the Belgian military aviation wing (*Aviation Militaire Belge*), and the pilots in question (Lt. Orta, Slt. Behaege and Slt. Castiaux) formed the squadron with two observers (Slt. Russchaert and Slt. Collignon), plus five NCOs acting as mechanics and craftsmen. As for the aircraft, they were Short Type 827s loaned by the Royal Naval Air Service. Fitted with a Sunbeam Nubian motor producing 150 horsepower, the seaplanes used by the Belgians on Lake Tanganyika had a maximum speed of 125km/h and a flying time of some four hours. A triangular keel fitted at the rear and steered using a vertical rudder, a float underneath the tail of the aircraft provided buoyancy when landing on water. On each side, the Short Type 827 had three-metre floats while two smaller floats could be found beneath the wings to provide stability when landing on a slant. Carrying a maximum load of some 1,000kg (1 ton), the Short 827 could also be armed with a Lewis .303 machine gun.[13]

Also known as the Short Admiralty Type 827, in December 1915 the three seaplanes numbered 3093, 3094 and 3095 were dismantled by the RANS and packed into eight crates. Two back-up engines, canvas, and spare parts were also packed and prepared for shipment, as were a wireless phone, electrical and woodworking equipment necessary for assembly and maintenance, plus 3,000 16 and 65-pound bombs. Ammunition destined for the *Force Publique*, 50,000 litres (11,000 gallons) of petrol and 1,000 litres (220 gallons) of oil completed the cargo.

The first step of the voyage saw the crates taken to Falmouth in Cornwall, where they were loaded on to the Belgian cargo ship *Anversville*, a vessel owned by the Belgian Maritime Company of the Congo, or *Compagnie Belge Royal Maritime du Congo* (CBMC). Leaving Falmouth on 7 January 1916, the *Anversville* made its way to La Rochelle, a port on France's Atlantic coast, it reached Boma on 4 February. Two days later, the cargo reached the Congolese port of Matadi, where a further three days later de Bueger and the

command the unit and to organise the transfer of the craft to Lake Tanganyika.

Named HMS *Mimi* and HMS *Toutou*, the boats fitted with by 100-horsepower engines embarked on a 10,000-mile journey just three weeks after Lee's plan had been approved. Leaving London on 29 May 1915, the boats were shipped firstly to Cape Town in South Africa, then by train to Elisabethville in Katanga via Bulawayo. Arriving on 26 July 1915, the boats were then hauled across another 146 miles (235kms) of Congolese mountains and valleys

A similar journey some 50 years later

By the end of August 1965, what was known as the Congo Crisis (1960–1967) was drawing to a close due to the combined actions of mercenary forces such as 5, 6 and 10 Commandos, a mercenary force of Cuban exiles and Europeans that constituted the Congolese Air Force, or *Force Aérienne Congolaise* (FAC), and the Armée Nationale Congolaise (ANC).[15] The Kwilu Rebellion having been put down by this time, and the Kivu Rebellion almost eliminated in the north-west of the Congo, there remained, nonetheless, a threat to Congolese sovereignty in the east of the country where forces under Laurent-Désiré Kabila still controlled large areas of the north-western portion of Lake Tanganyika. The area becoming a stronghold due to the arrival of Ugandan troops to support the so-called 'Simba', more reinforcements arrived in April 1965 in the shape of communist Cuban forces including Che Guevara. The rebel force was backed by a number of radical African and Middle Eastern countries including Algeria and the United Arab Republic, and ports such as Cairo were used as stopover points for the transfer of Soviet and Chinese weaponry destined firstly for Dar es Salaam, then Ujiji on the east bank of Lake Tanganyika. The weapons in question having followed former Arab slave routes, from Ujiji and smaller coastal villages in Tanzania, were brought across the lake to Kabila's forces.

CIA planners recognised that this transfer of weapons had to be terminated. In an effort to achieve this goal, it was decided that the CIA would recruit a naval crew from 5 Commando and that this new force would patrol the lake to stop the flow of weapons and also be used for the transportation of troops along the Congo's main arteries. A number of ageing Congolese vessels were acquired, but these lacked the speed needed for the interception of small fishing boats used for contact between Ujiji and rebel forces. Moreover, even if faster craft could be supplied, the crew needed to operate them was not readily available in the Congo.

In August 1965, the US State Department decided to implement a programme whereby two Swift boats and their Cuban exile crews would be transferred from carrying out maritime anti-Castro operations in the Caribbean Sea to Lake Tanganyika. The two Swifts were named the *Monty* and the *Gitana*. The problem facing CIA planners at JM/WAVE in Miami was how to bring two 50-foot vessels to the Congo without raising suspicions. The solution was that the two boats were to be sailed from their base at Monkey Point in Nicaragua *via* the Gulf of Mexico to the makers of the Swifts in Morgan City, Louisiana. Once this had been done, the maker, Sewart Seacraft, cut up the boats into three pieces, and from here they were transported across the Atlantic on C-124 Globemasters before being reassembled in the Congo by Sewart's employees. Fitted with three .50-calibre machine guns, one .30-calibre machine gun, and 57mm recoilless cannon, the Congolese Naval Force (*Force Navale Congolaise*) comprising 16 Cuban exiles and a radio operator slowed the transfer of weapons down to a trickle, and convinced Guevara that the Cuban revolution was not coming to Africa as he had planned. He left the Congo in early November 1965.

flight crew of 3093 (Behaeghe, Colignon) oversaw its loading on to a paddleboat destined for Stanleyville. The destination of the cargo set as Albertville, some 3,000 km (1,800 miles) away from Léopoldville, it was then transported either by train or paddleboat through Ponthierville, Kindu, and Kongolo. From here, it was shipped along the River Lualaba to Kabolo, with the final leg of the journey made by train to Albertville.[14]

While 3094 and 3095 were to make a similar journey during the early months of 1916, the Germans were to lose the *Kingani* on 26 December 1915 and the *Hedwig von Wissman* on 9 February

The reassembling of a Short Type 827 (serial number 3094) Note the floats underneath the tail and fuselage. (Documents du service photographique du Ministère des colonies belges)

1916 due to the actions of HMS *Mimi* and HMS *Toutou* operating alongside Belgian craft. The consequence of this action was that the *Graf von Götzen* was to seek the shelter of Kigoma, but nevertheless it remained a threat due to its firing and transport capabilities.

To counter this threat, Cdt. de Bueger began to look for a base from which his small air force could operate. The Bay of Burton facing Usumbura (now Bujumbura) in Burundi was rejected as it was too far from Albertville, so it was proposed that de Bueger set up operations on Lake Tungwe, some 30 kilometres from the River Lukaga. Its waters much calmer than those of Lake Tanganyika, Lake Tungwe was ideal as it was separated from the much larger lake only by a small strip of land. Now all that was needed was the construction of a canal so that supplies could be shipped from Lake Tanganyika to Lake Tungwe, and in April 1916 work was started by engineers of the *Force Publique* and members of indigenous populations residing in the area.[16] The setting up of the air base and the construction of the canal corresponded to the time Anglo-Belgian forces decided to launch a major offensive against German East Africa.

The Tabora Offensive

For around a year, the objective of Belgian military preparations had been to occupy parts of German-held territory in view of future peace agreements made between the two sides. The main effort of the *Force Publique* was directed towards occupying Ruanda (Rwanda) and Urundi (Burundi) and seeking to extend Belgian influence to reach the shores of Lake Victoria.[17]

When it came to implementing the strategy, the first stages of the plan consisted of dividing the Northern Brigade under Commandant Philippe Molitor into two groups. The first, consisting of four battalions, two batteries and a detachment of 500 troops from the *Force Publique* post at Kigezi (south-west Uganda) was to assemble at Lutobo (Uganda), then advance southwards towards Kigali (Ruanda). A second group under Commandant Rouling was to advance from Kibati (Belgian Congo) and meet German forces garrisoned at Sabeya (Rwanda). Meanwhile, the Southern Brigade commanded by Lt. Colonel Olsen was to assemble to the south of Lake Kivu. This brigade divided into three groups with the largest comprising three battalions. Its role was to gain control of the Russisi crossing

near Shangugu on the southern tip of Lake Kivu, then to move eastwards to Nyanza (Rwanda).[18]

The movement of Molitor's troops commencing on 25 April 1916, their first encounter with German troops occurred five days

General Molitor, commander of the Northern Brigade. (Author's collection)

The movement of Allied forces in German East Africa, 1916–1918. Movements of the FP are shown in black. (Map by Tom Cooper)

The *Mortier de 58 mm type 2* was the standard medium trench warfare mortar used in the First World War. Here, one is operated by *Force Publique* troops during the East Africa Campaign. (Collection VR)

EST AFRICAIN ALLEMAND (Occupation Belge)
Entrée des Troupes Belges à Tabora
(19 Sept., 1916)
DUITSCH OOST AFRIKA (Belgische Bezetting)
Introde der Belgische Troepen in Tabora
(19den Sept., 1916)

Troops of the *Force Publique* make their way into Tabora on 19 September 1916. (Open source)

knowing that von Lettow-Vorbeck had already disarmed the German vessel and had sent its cannon to be used by the army, or that this gun had been replaced by a wooden mock-up,[21] 3093 made a low-altitude run at the ship and dropped two 65-pound bombs from the cockpit and fired its Lewis gun at the fleeing crew members. Disaster was averted for 3093, for having had one of its floats pierced by a shot fired from the ailing *von Götzen* it had lost stability and was forced to land on the lake. Fortunately, the Belgian vessel *Le Vengeur* spotted distress flares sent by the downed plane and was able to tow it back to the base at Mtoa. While the squadron was subsequently sent to Kigoma after its fall to Belgian forces, as for the *von Götzen*, by the time Kigoma had been captured the Germans had sailed her south of Kigoma, filled her with sand and scuttled her. The ship's destination set as Katabe Bay, by mid-1916 Lake Tanganyika was firmly in the hands of the Anglo-Belgian coalition. After capturing Kigoma, and with Ujiji also under Belgian control, the next stage of the offensive was to advance on to Tabora in Tanzania. The most important administrative centre of central German East Africa, in early August 1916 both the Northern and Southern brigades were ordered to march eastwards to the town.

The Tanganyika Railway providing the Southern Brigade a relatively direct route to Tabora and the interior of Tanzania, two columns under the command of FP officers Thomas and Muller departed from bases in Ujiji, Kigoma and Ruchugi. Muller's first task was to secure the railway crossing over the Mlgarasi River some 35 miles (56 km) east, and on 10 August he sent one battalion along the railway while a second column was sent through Fumfu to approach the crossing from the south. Meeting little resistance from a German rearguard, by the 14 August Muller's force had crossed the Sindi River and had found the Mlgarasi crossing unmanned. On the other hand, Thomas sent one battalion into the valley of the lower Mlgarasi on 8 August while the bulk of his column moved along the railway on 10 and 12 August. His forces were assembled at Ruchugi on 16 August, and on reaching Ugombe on 24 August, Thomas sent a detachment to Kirulumo. On 26 August, this detachment was joined by Moulaert's force approaching from Kibwesa. The next target for the force was a German camp at Simbili some 80 miles (130km) eastwards.[22] The town of Katunde – some 30 miles (50km) south of Tabora – was also captured, as was the German-held railway

later at Kasibu. Progress slowed by downpours; it was two weeks later, on 5 May, that the column along with its porters reached Lake Muhazi (Rwanda). As German forces retreated from the Sabeya to be replaced by Rouling's troops, they pulled back to Nyanza. In the meantime, two battalions of the *Force Publique*'s 1st Regiment commanded by Commandant Muller marched north-eastwards on 4 May. Also impeded by heavy rain, Muller reached Nyagatara (Rwanda) on 10 May. German forces having also abandoned the area, Muller reached Nyanza one week later.[19] The columns of the Northern Brigade reaching Rwandan capital Kigali on 20 May, by the last day of July 1916 – a day when the Battle of the Somme was taking place – the Southern Brigade had crossed the Tanzanian border reaching Kigoma. On its way, it had occupied Usumbura on 6 June, Kitega on 16 June, and Kasulu one week later.

The Southern Brigade's successful advance on had been greatly assisted by the *Force Publique*'s Lake Detachment of Short 827s. After a number of setbacks including the breakdown of 3093 and 3094 crashing into tree trunk shortly after take-off,[20] at 1800 hours on 12 June Behaeghe and Collignon guided 3093 across Lake Tanganyika with the objective of attacking the *Graf von Götzen*. Without

The victory parade through Tabora shortly after German forces retreated south-eastwards towards Sikonge, Tanzania. (Author's collection)

Here, the *Force Publique* marches into Mahenge in September 1917. (Open source)

station at Usoke on 30 August. A counterattack organised by German Major Wahle was repelled on 2 September, while on 7 September another German attack on Usoke used a naval gun mounted on a train wagon. Both the FP and the *Schutztruppen* suffered heavy losses, but once again the Germans were pushed back.[23] With German resistance broken at Usole, the path was clear for an advance on Tabora. On 8 September, the Southern Brigade carried out attacks at Lulanguru, and between 10–12 September the Northern Brigade attacked Wahle's positions at Itaga, where the suffered heavy casualties. In the meantime, British forces commanded by South African Brigadier-General Crewe had made their way south-eastwards from British East Africa and were preparing to join the Belgians for a final push towards Tabora on 19 September. From 15–18 September, the German force shelled Northern Brigade positions set up around Itaga. A renewed Belgian attack was planned for 19 September, but on the night of 18–19 September German forces retreated south-eastwards towards Sikonge, and in the morning of 19 September the civilian authorities surrendered leaving Tabora in the hands of Belgian forces.

Force Publique officers gather after victory at Tabora. (Author's collection)

An 'Arc de Triomphe' was erected in Elisabethville to pay homage to soldiers of the 1st Regiment of the *Force Publique* that had fought and won the Battle of Tabora. Note that British flags also adorn a monument inscribed *"Honneur aux Braves"*, or "Honour to the Courageous". This symbolises the joint effort made by Anglo-Belgian forces. (Author's collection)

forces in Kamerun, and in German East Africa suffering over 2,600 casualties. The last of the Belgian forces withdrawing from the First World War after suffering heavy losses (84 dead) during the Mahenge Offensive, notwithstanding a demonstration that it was a formidable army, the *Force Publique* still had many challenges to face in the years to come. Indeed, British forces accused the FP of having committed atrocities including rape against civilian populations as it made its way through Rwanda and across Tanzania.[24] These accusations of war crimes weakening the Belgian position when it came to negotiations over the future of the former German colonies, efforts were made by the Belgian colonial authorities in the Congo to strengthen the FP and to reinforce its capacity to answer internal and external threats. On 10 May 1919, and under the overall command of Armand Christophe Huyghé (later Armand Huyghé de Mahenge in recognition of his efforts in the Mahenge Offensive), the FP was reorganised into two branches: the *troupes campées* were given the role of guarding the border while the *troupes en service territoriale* were tasked with maintaining public order throughout the Congo itself. To perform this role, battalions of the *troupes en service territoriale* were assigned to every provincial capital, with companies of troops stationed at each district headquarters.[25] As for Belgium, as one of the victors of war in East Africa, the League of Nations mandated it administrative control of Ruanda-Urundi on 22 July 1922, a mandate in place until 1962.

There were few major encounters involving the FP following the Battle of Tabora. Belgian forces took part in the Mahenge Offensive that began in the summer of 1917 as part of the much larger East Africa Campaign, and they were not involved in the Battle of Mahiwa in German East Africa (15–18 October 1917) that opposed troops of the German Empire and those of the British Empire, mainly from India, Nigeria, and South Africa. Neither were Belgian forces involved at the Battle of Ngomano (25 November 1917) that opposed Germans and the Portuguese. Inasmuch as the First World War in Africa is concerned though, the different components of the FP not only accomplished their role of impeding German entry into the Belgian Congo, but they also made an important contribution to the defence of Northern Rhodesia and the defeat of German

4
The Interwar Period: The Development of the Belgian Congo

As was the case for many who left Europe for life in the colonies, the Belgians who set up home in the Congo attempted to recreate the society they had just left. Residing in fast-developing urban agglomerations such as Léopoldville, Stanleyville or Elisabethville, shop owners, bank managers, headmasters, and lawyers enjoyed the benefits of a colonial system whose officials were eager to promote the construction of cinemas, restaurants, swimming pools, and golf clubs but also to promote Christianity through the construction of churches and religious missions in which Congolese children received primary education.

The realisation that the Congo possessed such an abundance of mineral resources drew thousands of Belgians and other Europeans to the Congo in the years before the Great War. In terms of developing an infrastructure adapted to transport minerals

to the exterior, however, the Belgian Congo only truly began to emerge as an economic powerhouse in the 1920s. This was due to a programme of reform implemented by Louis Frank of the Colonial Office. Frank's plan to restructure the Congo was drawn along two axes: one that would deal with societal aspects and the other with economic aspects.

As for these reforms, improving the Congo's agricultural and farming landscapes was another area that drew Frank's attention. This, he said, would enable the indigenous population to have access to more abundant and better-quality food. The growing of cotton was another option that Frank would put forward to government ministers. In his opinion, if a colony was to be successful it needed private companies that would provide specialist expertise. For this reason, Frank called upon the Special Committee of the Katanga and

Forminière. As well as owning lands destined for the mining sector, both held large tracts of land reserved for agricultural exploitation. Cotonco was yet another company seen as important in Frank's plans. The objective of reforming the Congo's socio-economic backdrop required a substantial increase in the number of qualified and unqualified workers. In addition to providing subsidies and bonuses to all sections of the Belgian population willing to come to the Congo, improving the lives of the country's native population also became a priority. This would be achieved by increasing the number of educational and medical facilities, and Belgian teachers and doctors were, therefore, also encouraged to move to the colony. When it came to the question of who would perform which duties in this restructured economy, due to its "current level of knowledge and its capabilities", according to Frank, the role of the indigenous population was to work in "technical" areas of industry. Those who were particularly intelligent could eventually become clerks or even medical assistants.[1]

Though Frank's comments can be interpreted as symptomatic of a form of ingrained racism, the concept of 'equality' between blacks and whites was virtually unknown. Rather, Belgian authorities believed that they if they were reaping the economic benefits of the exploitation of natural resources, they also had the duty of improving the lives of Africans. They should be taken from a society based on tribal rituals towards one based on Christianity and on a Western belief system. This paternalist approach is illustrated by the reforming of the Congolese educational system initiated in 1922. Primary education, it was thought, would more likely ensure a contented population and the introduction of secondary education would give the Congolese the possibility to work as nurses, mechanics, etc. From the mid-1920s, the state encouraged an increase in the number schools and put particular emphasis on religious education. In 1941, there were six state schools for the native Congolese; three state schools for Europeans; and over 5,200 mission schools for the native Congolese. Mission schools also existed for European children. Run by the Christian Brothers, the Marist Brothers, Salesian Fathers, and the English Baptist Missionary, these schools prepared students for technical schools operated by UMHK or by Lever.[2] Authorities were equally aware of the need to educate future tribal chiefs and set up a school in Buta in northern Congo. While there was no provision for the Congolese to enter the liberal professions or to attend university at that time, a series of reforms carried out in the 1920s and, again

The *Princesse Marie-José* arrives in Léopoldville on 12 February 1925. A Handley Page W8f Hamilton, it had the distinction of becoming the world's first airliner to have on-board sanitation facilities. The aircraft was named after Marie-José of Belgium, the last Queen of Italy. (Author's collection)

The Georges Levy GL 40 HB2 was a three-seat hydroplane first produced in France in 1917. Designed by Maurice Jules-Marie Le Pen, and nicknamed the "flying coffin", the Levy-Lepen was used by several air forces of the time including Finland, Portugal, and the United States. The example pictured here is undergoing testing in the Belgian Congo. (Author's collection)

in the 1930s, saw the emergence of a middle-class Congolese elite holding jobs that were relatively well paid. Inasmuch as industrial infrastructure, although the *Compagnie du Chemin de Fer du Congo* (CCFC) had completed a functioning network of rail links by 1898, Frank had the vision of extending this network into the far reaches of the Congo in order to "spread civilisation and to exploit the economic opportunities that the Congo had to offer".[3] Not a supporter of fully state-owned enterprises, the plan was to partially privatise the network to encourage investment. The railway system was not the only economic infrastructure concerned by the reforms: Frank wanted to revitalise the Congo's ports, make Katangan mines more productive, and provide the means for the province's copper to be transported across the Kasaï to the Atlantic Ocean. Waterways were equally important to economic development. Organised river transport had begun as early as 1881 with the *Marine du Haut Congo* operating steamers, and in 1925 this company merged with the *Union Nationale des Transports Fluviaux* (UNATRA). Over the

coming years, the union was absorbed by the *Office d'Exploitation des Transports Coloniaux* (OTRACO).

The Development of Commercial Aviation in the Belgian Congo (1920s and 1930s)

On 26 June 1919, Albert I of Belgium issued a royal decree that led to the setting up of a research committee whose role was to study the future of aviation in the Belgian Congo. Financed by money from a *Fonds Spécial*,[4] the role of the *Comité d'Etudes pour la Navigation Aérienne au Congo* (CENAC) was twofold. Firstly, and with a budget of some two million francs, the committee was to establish an airline capable of carrying passengers and mail between Stanley Pool and Stanleyville; second, the committee was to examine the possibility of mapping the Congo River using aerial photography. To achieve these objectives, the CENAC turned towards a contractor the *Syndicat Nationale pour l'Etude des Transports Aériens* (SNETA),[5] with this entity working within the limits and instructions of the CENAC.[6] SNETA, itself, had been financed and created on 25 March

The de Havilland DH.50 was a single-engined biplane first manufactured in Britain and built under license in Belgium. First used to provide a link between the Belgian Congo's major cities, it was replaced by the Handley Page W8f. (alchetron)

The Breguet 19A1 with Edmond Thieffry arrives at Léopoldville on 21 March 1926. (Author's collection)

A member of the *Force Publique* at a ceremony celebrating Thieffry's flight. (Author's collection)

Capable of reaching a speed of 90mph (145km/h), these seaplanes could carry a load of 880lbs (400kg) for four hours non-stop. In addition, SNETA was provided with a dozen Bessonneau canvas hangars, and pilots and technicians from the Belgian military were given authorisations to enter and work in the Belgian Congo. Lastly, the Belgian Congo's authorities put its marine workshops in Léopoldville at SNETA's disposal.[7]

After testing was carried out, in August 1919 the Belgian personnel left Europe and arrived at Stanley Pool towards the end of September. Setting up the hangars and finding suitable locations for stopover points were some of the difficulties encountered by the Belgian aviation delegation. However, their mission was provided with assistance from local authorities who purchased private land to serve as airfields and put soldiers of the FP's engineering division in Léopoldville at the mission's disposal. These soldiers were given the job of clearing fields and woods so that accommodation and offices for the new airline service could be constructed. The slipways needed to bring the aircraft from their hangars to the sometimes-steep slopes of the Congo River were often crafted on the spot, while the construction of the hangars was also problematic due to some of their parts having been lost in transit. Another problem was the high winds that blew along the Congo. The hangars were sufficiently moored to survive them, but the canvas awnings did not survive the effects of the sun. These were then replaced by tarred wooden planks. As for fuel, the fear that it would evaporate led the mission to dig underground storage rooms. Notwithstanding these difficulties, an airline christened the *Ligne Aérienne du Roi Albert* (LARA), or the King Albert Airline was established with the first service provided in July 1920 between Léopoldville and N'Gombe with a stopover at Bololeo. N'Gombe was chosen due to its proximity to its position at the confluence of the Congo and Oubanghi rivers. Next, in December 1920, the second section was opened with the service providing a link between N'Gombe and Mobeka (stopover at Coquilhatville). The third, launched in June 1921, linked Lisala and Stanleyville.[8]

As LARA continued to operate one of the world's first commercial airlines, a number of further difficulties connected to the climatic conditions in the Congo began to influence the aircraft. By June

1919 by the *Banque d'Outremer*, a bank dealing with the funding of projects overseas.

The first steps made towards the setting up of the link between Stanley Pool and Stanleyville were made in Brussels when 12 Levy-Lepen seaplanes with spares were placed at the disposal of SNETA.

The record-breaking DH.88 Comet at N'Dolo. Pilot 'Teddy' Franchomme was a fighter pilot with the 5th 'Comet' squadron during the First World War. (Delcampe)

The Fokker F.VII named in honour of Thieffry. Produced by Dutch aircraft manufacturer Fokker, SABENA possessed 28 of these three-engined airliners with five making the link between Belgium and the Congo. As well as the *Edmond Thieffry*, SABENA operated the *Léopold Roger* (OO-AGI), and Fokker F. VIIbs serial-numbered OO-AGG, OO-AGJ, and OO-AGK. (Belgianwings)

The realisation that air transport within the Congo and between Belgium and its African colonies offered numerous economic benefits soon led to the creation of the *Société Anonyme Belge d'Exploitation de la Navigation Aérienne* (SABENA) in 1923. SABENA operated flights between the Congo and Europe.[12] One of the worlds' first commercial airline companies, though the airline was partly funded by Belgians in the Congo, the man behind the project to link Brussels to Léopoldville by air was Edmond Thieffry. A former member of the *Compagnie des Ouvriers et Aérostiers,* or Belgian Army Air Corps (BAAC), Thieffry obtained permission from the Belgian government to fly a Handley Page W8f Hamilton (registered O-BAHO) named the *Princesse*

1922, LARA was operating twice-monthly flights in each direction employing 30 Europeans and 250 Congolese,[9] but the plywood hulls of the Levy-Lepen were absorbing too much water and causing glue to ferment. As the glue expanded it created blisters, and these pockets of air often began to separate the layers of wood making up the hull. Secondly, and although the 300 HP Renault engines adapted well to the heat of the Congo, what kept maintenance teams busy was the overheating of the radiator. This was deemed too small and was only able to maintain the water at 80°c (176°f). Though efforts to replace the Levy-Lepens came with LARA operating the three-engined Handley Page W8f Hamilton,[10] LARA's operations were discontinued on 7 June 1922.[11]

Marie-José between the Belgian and Congolese capitals. Leaving on 12 February 1925 from Haren airport in Brussels, the flight plan called for stops in France, Algeria, Mali, Chad, the Central African Republic and Coquilhatville before making the final leg of the journey to Léopoldville. Though the flight was provisionally planned to take only seven days, strong adverse winds and a broken propeller meant that, finally, it took 51 days with the aircraft reaching Léopoldville on 3 April 1925. Nonetheless, the link had been made, Thieffry became a Belgian hero, and regular flights between Brussels and Léopoldville were to become the norm. Effectively, the realisation that flights between Belgium and the Congo could be made over much shorter periods came in March 1926 when a

Some of SABENA's fleet of Fokker F.VIIs pictured at N'Dolo. (Author's collection)

A Savoia-Marchetti S.73 pictured at N'Dolo. (Belgianwings)

Breguet 19A1 flown by lieutenants George Madaets, Jean Verhaegen and Adjutant Joseph Coppens made the 5,600-mile (9,000km) trip in 12 days. The aircraft named the *Reine Elisabeth* and equipped with a Hispano-Suiza engine, its voyage led to the construction of aerodromes that began in the Congo in 1926, and the first regular air service between Europe and Central Africa. Indeed, SABENA began to operate flights between Boma, Léopoldville and Elisabethville (Lubumbashi) the same year.[13]

The development of commercial flight in the Belgian Congo 1930s was very much a continuation of what had been started in the 1920s, and very much part of an international competition to find out which aircraft manufacturer could develop the fastest aircraft. The Great Depression somewhat limited SABENA's expansion, but 1934 was to witness a record-breaking run from Brussels to Léopoldville in 1934. Named in honour of Queen Astrid, the wife of Léopold III, a two-seat, twine-engined DH.88 Comet (registered G-ACSR) piloted by Lt.-Colonel Maurice 'Teddy' Franchomme and Briton Ken Waller set off from the Belgian military airport at Haren (aka Evere) on 20 December 1934 bound for N'Dolo. Some 44 hours and 15 minutes of flight time later, it landed at Haren after having delivered Christmas mail and having attained an average speed of 202mph (326km/h).

The Fokker F. VIIb/3m was to be at the forefront of SABENA's operations from 1935 when the airline inaugurated a regular passenger service between Belgium and the Congo. The inaugural flight taking place in February 1935, a Fokker named in honour of Edmond Thieffry (serial number OO-AGH) carried three crew and one passenger. The name of this passenger being Tony Orta, it will be remembered that he had taken part in air operations on Lake Tanganyika from 1915 aboard a Short 827. Developments continued with the construction of SABENA's Guest House in 1937– lodgings later used by CIA pilots during the Congo Crisis – and by the end of 1938 SABENA was celebrating its 100th flight between mainland Europe and Central Africa. By this time SABENA was operating the German-made Junkers Ju 52, and the Italian-made Savoia-Marchetti S.73P. The replacement of the F.VII by the Savoia-Marchetti in October 1936 came in spite of the crash of S.73 (registered OO-AGN) operated by SABENA between Haren and Croydon Airport in December 1935 killing 11 people. The more powerful S.83 monoplane was also envisaged for use in 1938.

5

The Belgian Congo and the Second World War

The Political Context

Having confronted several challenges from tribal organisations in the early 1930s – the most important being the Pende Revolt of 1931 in which government troops killed up to 550 members of the tribe – and challenges relating to the internal organisation of the FP and the quality of its recruits,[1] the next major operations in which the Belgian Congo's military forces were involved occurred during the Second World War. As for the First World War, the authorities in the Belgian Congo were keen to maintain the colony's neutrality so as it would not be drawn into a second conflict, this time fought against Nazi Germany. This it managed to do until 10 May 1940 when Germany invaded Belgium and had taken a mere 18 days to complete its occupation of the country.

The international position of the Belgian Congo at the outbreak of a second global conflict had stabilised during the 1920s and 1930s despite a degree of tribal manifestations designed to demonstrate opposition to the conditions of colonial rule. The Belgian Congo had survived the First World War; economically, the colony was thriving due to its exports of valuable mineral resources; and for the most important colonising nations of Great Britain and France, it was better for them to have the Belgian Congo as a neighbour rather than one seeking to extend an empire by encroaching recognised territorial boundaries. In regards to the allies of the Belgian Congo in Africa, some tensions remained: there was the attitude of London towards the Congo Free State; disagreements that had arisen during the First World War (accusations of brutality against the *Force Publique*); and the fear that Britain itself would use its positional strength in Southern Africa in an attempt to gain more influence in Katanga, a province highly valued by the British for economic reasons. Brussels, therefore, remained vigilant as to British objectives in southern and central Africa, even preferring that German East Africa not go to Great Britain but to another country such as Italy.[2] Although not to the same extent, the Belgian Congo was also wary of French plans in central Africa including the construction of a railway line from Brazzaville to Pointe Noire in French Congo that was competing for trade with the Léopoldville-Matadi line. For this reason, the authorities in the Belgian Congo as well as in Brussels reinforced ties with Portugal.[3]

Considering Belgium's earlier preferences for Italy to have played a more significant role in the dividing up of German East Africa, it is paradoxical that Italy under Benito Mussolini and neither France nor Great Britain that had the greatest influence over the *Force Publique*'s military operations in the Second World War. It has been documented that Great Britain had no intention of letting the Congo fall into German hands and was prepared to breach previous agreements concerning the Congo's territorial integrity, and it has been documented that France, angered by Belgium's surrender on 28 May 1940, was prepared to send troops to occupy Léopoldville.[4] What changed this geopolitical game of chess, and changed the immediate future however was France's surrender in June 1940. The Belgian government, concerned about developments in Western Europe, gave the Minister of Colonies, Albert de Vleeschauwer, full legislative and executive power to administer the colony as he thought best.[5] Though still worried about British attitudes towards Katanga in particular, there were a number of elements that finally pushed the Belgian Congo into siding with Great Britain. Effectively, De Vleeschauwer was warned that the British government was preparing to recognise a group of left-wing politicians in London as the Belgian government in exile.[6] This group led by radicals Marcel-Henri Jaspar, Camille Huysmans and Isabelle Blume were making attempts to gain recognition for their *Comité national belge*, or Belgian National Committee (BNC), but these were thwarted when De Vleeschauwer arrived in London in early July 1940 to meet with senior British officials including Churchill, and offered Great Britain the Congo's financial assistance.[7] Eventually, De Vleeschauwer, Camille Gutt (Finance Minister), Paul-Henri Spaak (Foreign Affairs), and Hubert Pierlot (Prime Minister) formed the "Government of Four" and became the Belgian government in exile. It was to receive full diplomatic recognition from the Allies and was to be based in London for the remainder of the war. During this time, the government in exile oversaw the operations of the Free Belgian Forces, it loaned Belgium's gold reserves to Great Britain and the United States,[8] and it was responsible for the affairs of the Belgian Congo. This included placing the colony's raw materials at the disposal of the Allies including the mines at Shinkolobwe in Katanga. Here, UMHK mined uranium-235, a strain of uranium that was used by scientists working on the Manhattan Project. They would use it to develop the atom bombs dropped on Hiroshima and Nagasaki, namely *Little Boy* and *Fat Man*.

The Military Involvement of the *Force Publique* in the

Second World War

As was the case with the First World War, the bulk of the fighting involving the FP took place in East Africa where the Belgian Congo's armed forces waged war against Italy, its colony of Italian East Africa, and fought alongside troops from the UK, South Africa, British India, Uganda, Kenya, Somaliland, West Africa, France (Free French), Northern and Southern Rhodesia, Sudan, and Nyasaland. Mussolini having proclaimed the formation of Italian East Africa on May 1936, just over four years later on 10 June 1940, he declared war on Britain and France, thereby threatening their colonies in East Africa and important shipping lanes in the Gulf of Aden, the Red Sea, and the Suez Canal.

Though there was a certain degree of hesitancy from Congolese Governor General Pierre Ryckmans as to how the Belgian Congo should react to this declaration of war – after all, Italy had not declared war on Belgium – initial doubts on what role the FP should play were to be transformed into convictions on 19 November 1940 when it was learnt that Italian planes used to bomb London had taken off from Belgium. The Government of Four declaring that a state of war existed between Belgium and Italy on 23 November, Ryckmans then declared that the Belgian Congo was also at war against the Italians and mobilised the FP.

It was in some ways fortunate that the Belgian Congo was distanced from conflict taking place in the Mediterranean and in the North Atlantic. It meant that the Congo itself was unlikely to become a major battlefield of the Second World War, even if Katanga represented a very valuable trophy but, at the same time, the Congo's occupation of a lower rung on the geopolitical ladder meant that the supplying of better weapons to the Force Publique remained a low priority for the Allies. Moreover, the potential for the officers of the *Force Publique* was weakened as many of Belgium's best were attracted by the possibility of training to become a pilot in the South African Air Force (SAAF), or the RAF.[9]

As far as the question of distance from the major theatres of war, De Vleeschauwer did have some concerns about the possibility of a German naval attack on Boma, despite the nearest U-boat activity taking place thousands of miles away in Sierra Leone or around the southern cape (Boma giving access to the larger port of Matadi and access to the Congo's interior through the country's rail network). Certainly, the armaments found at the fort of Shinkakasa provided some form of protection, but De Vleeschauwer wanted Britain to provide more naval guns, torpedo boats, aircraft and anti-aircraft artillery to counter the threat of invasion starting at the mouth of the Congo River.[10] A more plausible area of the Congo for Axis powers to launch an attack on the Belgian Congo did, however, exist in the northeast, and Stanleyville was identified as the most likely target. Should the Italians choose to advance on this city in the Oriente Province, the quickest way to reach their destination was to cut across the southern tip of the Anglo-Egyptian Sudan.

Up to late November 1940, with Belgium not at war with Italy, no Congolese troops were authorised to fight outside the Congo despite the fears mentioned above. Belgium's declaration of war against Italy on 27 November completely changed the circumstances, however, but an issue for military strategists at the British East Africa Command felt that the *Force Publique* lacked the training and weapons to assume offensive action. More suited to the defence of the Belgian Congo, one battalion of the *Force Publique* was, nonetheless, authorised to garrison in the Sudan.[11]

In many respects, British concerns about the *Force Publique*'s readiness for offensive action were valid: the 39,000 members of the Congo's armed forces (15,000 troops and 24,000 porters) were

The Mle. 1889 was gradually replaced by the Mle. 89/36. Here, an FP soldier is trained to use the rifle circa 1943. The rifle used a Mauser-style bolt action and had a five-round internal magazine. As standard, the rifle was affixed with an M1924 bayonet. (Open source)

The Bofors-designed L/60 40mm short-range AA gun was designed in the 1930s by Swedish manufacturer AB Bofors. It was used by most Allied forces in the Second World War. (Author's collection)

in use were the Mle. 1889, the FN Mle. 89/36, the Mle. 1903 pistol and, as standard in the Second World War, the FN GP-35. After the war, this pistol was replaced by the Browning 9mm Hi-Power. As for field artillery, the FP was still using the Saint-Chamond, a 75mm French-made gun, but had updated its arsenal to include a modified version of the Mle. 1897 *Soixante-Quinze* (modified 1938). The FP's most modern artillery piece was the British-supplied Ordnance QF 25-Pounder Mk. II that were to be used by FP in Abyssinia. Air defences consisted of the British-supplied Bofors 40mm anti-aircraft cannon and the Vickers QF 3.7-inch AA gun. Lastly, the FP possessed several Minerva armoured cars. Despite its obvious military shortcomings, by the time the *Force Publique* was fully mobilised in March 1941, whatever support it could offer to British-led forces commanded by Field Marshall Archibald Wavell was welcome.

Cooperation between Great Britain and Belgium was officialised on 21 January 1941 with the signing of a Financial and Purchase Agreement that was to last for the duration of the war. Under this two-part agreement, Britain agreed to support the Congolese economy while, at the same time, taking advantages of preferential trading terms for the Congo's raw materials such as gold, copper, cotton and copal, a tree resin used in varnishes. For the second part of the agreement, one of a military nature, Congolese forces would join up with Allied forces fighting in Abyssinia, a part of Italian East Africa that British commanders had identified as central to strategies designed to defeat Italian forces. The British-commanded forces consisting of the 1st South Africa Division, the 11th and 12th Africa Divisions (British colonial forces made up of West and East African troops commanded by British, South African, and Rhodesian officers), the plans for Abyssinia included advancing on Addis Ababa in the hope of spurring native Abyssinians in the south of the country to rebel against the Italians.

concentrated into three groups in different areas of the Congo; the displacement of these troops plus logistical planning and communications were difficult due to the size of the Congo; and as for weapons, during the 1930s the FP had gradually become a military force intended for use on the border, or to maintain order within the Congo. Subsequently, the FP lacked field artillery, tanks, aircraft, anti-aircraft weaponry, and there was a complete absence of troops trained for airborne operations. Importantly, what weapons the FP did possess were obsolete. Indeed, the rifles and pistols still

The Mle. 1897 *Soixante-Quinze* (or *Canon de 75 modèle 1897*) is widely regarded as the first modern artillery piece. Designed as an anti-personnel weapon, in the First World War, it was used to fire time-fused shrapnel shells or impact-detonated high-explosive shells. By the end of the First World War, it had become the main means of firing toxic gas shells. (Author's collection)

FP fusiliers leave for Abyssinia in January 1941. (Author's collection)

uninhabitable, and after several weeks marching through the jungles, swamps and deserts of the Congo it was inevitable that cases of dysentery brought on by a lack of hygiene would slow down the advance of the FP and kill or severely weaken many hundreds. Nevertheless, progress was made, and thoughts were to turn with reaching Asosa in the Sudan, a settlement situated some 300 miles (480km) north of the Italian headquarters at Saïo. Setting off from Watsa in the north-east of the Congo, the 1st Battalion crossed the Congo-Sudan border and descended by way of Yei to Juba. This city situated at the head of the White Nile; the column then headed northwards towards Malakal before turning eastwards at Melut. Next, under the command of Commandant Isidore Herbiet it headed towards Kurmuk, just outside Asosa. Here, preparations were made for a joint attack made with soldiers of the King's African Rifles (KAR) commanded by Colonel William Johnson. Situated in the western extremity of the Sudan, Asosa served as a base for 1,500 men of the Italian 10th Brigade, and it possessed a radio station, a hospital and an aerodrome.[12] The combined attack of the FP and the KAR commenced on 11 March 1941, around six weeks after the FP had left Stanley Pool. On reaching Asosa, the joint force was somewhat surprised to find that the Italians had fled. No losses were suffered by either Belgian or British forces. After Asosa, the 1st Battalion – comprising 700 men and 400 porters – doubled back 225 miles (360km) across the Sudanese desert to the port of Melut, then eastward and parallel to the Sobat and Baro rivers. The Baro a tributary of the Nile and defining part of the border between the Sudan and Abyssinia, the FP then advanced towards an Italian garrison situated in the town of Gambela, an important river port used for the transport of coffee and other goods from Abyssinia to Egypt.

The Italians knowing that retreat would force them up the hills to Saïo they put up a stiff resistance. They placed machine guns under sycamore trees along the river making attack by water impossible, and they also set up a second line of machine guns to cover the road into Gambela. More were placed on the peak of a conical hill overlooking the town.[13]

The task facing Congolese forces leaving Stanley Pool in early 1941 was immense due to the vast distance that had to be covered. The first target for the FP being the market town of Saïo (currently Dembidolo) in south-western Abyssinia, the troops of the FP had to make their way across 2,000 miles of central Africa. The journey made using roads, rail and waterways, the first leg consisted of travelling the 1,000 miles from Stanley Pool to Aketi (formerly Port-Chaltin) by barge. The next stop was Mungbere in the Haut-Uele Province, and from here the FP made its way to Juba in the Sudan (now South Sudan) by rail. The last stage of the journey was to see the FP transported along the waters of the White Nile before crossing western Sudan and encountering the Italians at their base at Saïo, a town situated over 5,600 ft above sea level.

The journey across the Congo proved to be treacherous enough in itself. The 6,000 troops plus 4,000 porters had to deal with searing heat, a lack of fresh water, lands that were uninhabited/

FP troops faced a gruelling journey across the Congo and the Sudan before reaching Abyssinia. (Open source)

next part of the strategy was to defeat the concentration of 7,000 Italian troops commanded by General Carlo De Simone at Saïo. Replaced shortly after by General Pietro Gazzera, both knew that the hills surrounding Saïo offered a certain degree of protection and that the rainy season would hamper attempts to launch an offensive. Nevertheless, forces commanded by Lt. Colonel Van der Meersch were ordered to attack on 15 April, and this attack took place at Bortai Brook. Lt. Simonet of the FP's 6th Battalion was killed in battle while a former Legionnaire Sgt. Dorgeo was shot after stumbling into an Italian ambush. A Congolese corporal and four Congolese infantrymen also lost their lives. As for the opposing forces, they lost three Italians and 40 Eritreans, while 70 were wounded.[14] Nine days later, on 24 April, the troops of the FP were pounded by Italian cannons. This resulted in the retreat of the FP with soldiers falling back to their lines.

For much of May and the first half of June 1941, the beginning of the rainy season in Abyssinia meant that Belgian forces were bogged down and that their supply routes were virtually cut off. Many died after contracting Beriberi, but the second half of June saw an improvement in climatic conditions, and somewhat paradoxically, the rains assisted the FP in that the waters of the Sobat and Baro had swelled meaning that food, ammunition, and reinforcements could be brought from the Congo to the troops at Saïo via the White Nile.

With the reinforcements in place, FP strategy consisted of isolating Gazzera's forces by attacking their supply chain at Mogi, another town situated on the plateau near Saïo. The with SAAF also joining in with the effort by sending Fairey-Hartebeest biplanes to patrol and strafe Saïo, by 3 July the FP troops now under General Auguste-Edouard Gilliaert felt buoyed and ready for action. That morning, FP advanced posts opened fire on Italian positions, artillery was used by the FP to dampen the spirits of their opponents, and under the command of Commandant Duperoux, a battalion left base camp and went forward from base camp to flank the hills on which Saïo was perched. Simultaneously, a second advance saw Van der Meersch's 3rd Battalion make a sweeping movement across the plateau to surprise the Italian forces. Some of them retreated under heavy fire from the FP's artillery, and early in the afternoon of 3 July it was the turn of the Italian generals. They were seen aboard two Mitalia vehicles making their way down from Saïo, and with them they brought Gazzera's offer of surrender.[15] The terms of his surrender accepted by Gilliaert on 6 July, the FP captured thousands of Italian troops including eight generals; 7,600 rifles; 330 pistols; 15,000 grenades; 200 machine guns; 18 cannons; and 250 transport vehicles. While one source puts FP losses at 500,[16] another states that only four Belgian soldiers were killed and six seriously injured during the assault on Saïo. Throughout the Abyssinian campaign, 193 native FP soldiers lost their lives to illness while 2,328 porters also died from exhaustion or dysentery.

The surrender of Italian forces at Saïo put an end to their resistance in the Galla Sidamo region of Abyssinia and combined with British victory over a larger Italian force at Amba Alagi in May, it also ended Italian advances in East Africa. The FP returned to base in November 1941, and as had been the case with the defeat of German forces at Tabora in the First World War, defeat of Italian forces was widely celebrated. Indeed, it was Belgium's first victory since its capitulation to Nazi Germany. For the soldiers of the *Force Publique* that remained in the Belgian Congo itself, the remainder of the Second World War consisted of ensuring the territorial duties befitting those of a constabulary.

However, as far as the FP was concerned, its contribution to the Allied war effort continued abroad reaching far-off destinations such

The 1st Battalion of the FP was joined by soldiers from the 2nd/6th KAR who had defeated Italian forces at Afodu in early March, the first objective of attacks launched on 22 March was to silence the machine gun nests situated on the banks of the river. The next target was to take control of the hill, and to reach this goal infantrymen with fixed bayonets were ordered into battle. Now dominant, the joint Anglo-Belgian forces finally dispatched the remaining machine gun posts while the remainder of the Italian troops fled towards Saïo. Three Belgian infantrymen were killed during the attacks and 18 were wounded. More soldiers were lost the next day when two Caproni bombers attacked Gambela. The area around Gambela now firmly under control of Allied forces, the

Soldiers of the FP were fortunate enough to have made part of the journey by train. (Author's collection)

FP gunners man artillery used in an attack on Italian forces in July 1941. (Open source)

as Burma. Indeed, in July 1942, 13,000 FP troops were sent to Nigeria to prepare for a planned invasion of the Vichy France-held Dahomey (now Benin). The invasion cancelled,[17] the brigade was then sent to serve in the Middle East after travelling 6,000 miles from Zaria in Northern Nigeria to Cairo; the FP was then stationed along the Suez Canal where its troops guarded Prisoners of War, roads and storage facilities; in April 1944 the FP helped quell fighting between royalist and communist forces in Greece and between September 1944 and January 1945 the FP assumed duties in Palestine. Concurrently, the FP mounted field hospitals in Madagascar, India and in Burma.[18] This medical mission consisted of 370 men of the 10th Belgian Congo Casualty Clearing Station supporting the 11th East African Division who were involved in fighting the Japanese.

6

Aviation in the Belgian Congo, 1940–1944

The Origins of the *Force Publique*'s Air Wing

The annexation of Austria then the Sudeten by Nazi Germany in the first months of 1938 alerted Belgian officials to the reality that the Second World War could extend beyond Europe's borders and affect Africa. Albert de Vleeschauwer was to raise the question of protecting Belgium's colony by guarding the mouth of the Congo in November 1939 and the declaration of war with Italy, but even as parts of Czechoslovakia became occupied one of De Vleeschauwer's predecessors as Minister of the Colonies, Paul Crockaert was giving similar warnings and encouraging the use of aircraft to patrol the Congo's Atlantic coast lest Germany choose this route as a means of attaining the inner reaches of central Africa. Crockaert also remarked that a danger existed not just in south-western areas of the Congo, but also in the north-east where there was a risk of invasion from enemy forces. For this reason, he advocated the use of float planes as a means of warding off attack in the Great Lakes region as the Belgian Congo had done in 1915. Moreover, Crockaert judged that it was indispensable for the authorities in the colony to set up a system whereby the FP was substantially reinforced and armed. In his mind, the presence of a powerful air force would play an essential role.[1] This was an attempt to underline the reality that the *Force Publique* was woefully ill-equipped to confront an enemy force and that what war material it did possess was not adapted to the requirements of modern warfare. It lacked munitions, heavy weaponry, had no logistics or medical branch and possessed no aviation. In short, the FP in 1938 was incapable of performing its mission correctly. Efforts were subsequently made to bolster the numbers of men serving within the *Force Publique* including a recruitment campaign that would double the number of soldiers in the Congo from 15,000 to 30,000. Organised into three brigades based in the Lower Congo, Katanga, and the north-eastern territories respectively, during the so-called 'phoney war', De Vleeschauwer, however, noting that there were budgetary restraints refused to mobilise Congolese troops and

acted only when Belgium was defeated in May 1940. This refusal was symbolic of a long line of disputes between civilian and military authorities that hampered efforts to reform the *Force Publique* in the late 1930s. Notwithstanding this refusal, Colonel Emile Hennequin, the Commander of the FP and predecessor to Auguste Gilliaert made a separate appeal to the Belgian government whereby he called for the creation of a colonial aviation force that would act as support to the three FP brigades, and would subsequently serve in three areas of the Congo. The section based in the Lower Congo would also be responsible for maritime operations including reconnaissance. The "Hennequin Plan" was presented to the Belgian Minister for Colonies. The plan appears to have been greeted favourably, as in February 1940 Major Lucien Leboutte was seconded to the General Staff of the FP in order to carry out an appraisal of the aeronautical infrastructure already in place, and to weigh up how it could be developed to assist the FP. Leboutte's mission was interrupted by the advent of the Second World War leaving the FP with nothing but three single-engined aircraft intended for tourism.

Meanwhile, on 12 May 1940, the 5th Squadron of the Pilot Training Academy based in Wevelgem, Belgium was ordered to move any aircraft in its use to Tours in France. The aircraft that had not been destroyed by the Luftwaffe were first flown to Amiens, then Chartres, while ground crew made their way by train through the western parts of Belgium's southerly neighbour. Finally, the last destination for these aircraft and maintenance personnel was Caen-Carpiquet airfield in Normandy, which was reached on 20 May 1940, the same day the commanders of the training academy were told that the new centre for pilot instruction would be Oudja in north-eastern Morocco. To reach Oujda, the 50 or so Stampe-Vertongen SV.4, Avro 504, Fairey Fox, and Koolhovens used by the academy were dismantled and loaded on to a cargo ship named the *Algérie*, a vessel which had been provided by French authorities. The cargo's first stop Marseille, it was placed on to two smaller ships and

A Stampe-Vertongen SV.5 Tornado (serial number S-27) of the BAF's pilot training academy has a rocky landing. The date is unknown but the SV.5 was used by the BAF from 1936/1937 to 1940. (Belgianwings)

Franz Burniaux was one of 44 Belgians who served with the SAAF in the Second World War. He retired as Lieutenant General in the Belgian Air Force. (Open source)

set sail for Oran in Algeria on 28–29 May. The plan being for the training academy and the remnants of Belgium's air force to travel from Morocco to the Belgian Congo, events taking place in France at this time that were to interfere with plans. France signing an armistice with Nazi Germany on 24 June and leaving French North Africa in the hands of the Vichy Regime, Belgian General Tapproge had had the foresight to requisition seven Savoia-Marchetti 73s operated by SABENA and to base them in Algeria. The next stage of the plan was to use the SM.73s as transporters and as supply planes,

French military authorities initially objected to the plan and used the pretext that there was not enough fuel available at the different refuelling points situated at French-controlled bases between Oujda and the Congo. Moreover, with Italy having joined the Axis on 10 June, its authorities also had a say in what happened to Belgian material now in Algeria. The SV.73s were confiscated by the Italians even though Italy and Belgium were not at war.

For many of the pilots in training, or those that had been recalled to serve in the Belgian Air Force (BAF), the only thought on their mind was to return to Belgium. However, the Belgian government was in disarray at its new headquarters in Limoges, France; the commanders of the BAF were based in Montpellier on France's Mediterranean coast, so travelling to Great Britain or to the Belgium Congo under their own steam became an option for any flyer who wished to continue the battle. With that, on 3 July 1940 around 60 trainees and pilot instructors boarded a train to Casablanca. Most would choose to travel aboard a ship bound for Cardiff via Gibraltar, while the remainder attempted to make their way to Léopoldville. This group included Franz Burniaux and Gérard Greindl, two pilots who would later enrol in the SAAF and who would both be awarded the Distinguished Flying Cross (DFC) for their actions in combat.

Their voyage to South Africa starting in Casablanca with stopovers in Lisbon, Madeira, and Matadi, two days after their arrival in the Congo on 17 December 1940, Burniaux met with Colonel Gilliaert at the FP's HQ. A senior officer who had fought in the Congo in the First World War, and an officer with enough experience to witness how valuable air power was to the overall war effort, Gilliaert regretted that Belgium's colonial troops were about to be sent to Abyssinia without any aviation to provide transport or cover. As was the case with General Hennequin, what Gilliaert wanted was to create an air wing for the *Force Publique* that would serve these purposes. Though Gilliaert underestimated how difficult it would be to implement the logistics and technology needed to bring his plans to fruition, he wanted to resurrect Hennequin's plan. To achieve this, he asked Burniaux to open an "aviation" office at FP HQ, to make an inventory of what equipment was available, to draw up plans for an aviation capable of reconnaissance and of providing a support role, and to put in place the means for recruiting air crew. The details of the plan were to be ready in five to six weeks and were to be presented to De Vleeschauwer. Drawing up a list of what aircraft could be put into service did not take long. Consisting of three S.73Ps, a Fokker F.VII and six Ju 52/3ms, two Lockheed Model 14 Super Electras (Lockheed 14) used by the French had been seized by Belgian authorities at Elisabethville as a reprisal for the confiscation of the S.73s in Algeria some months earlier. The list was presented to Vleeschauwer in early February 1941, with Burniaux also submitting requirements for what aircraft he believed constituted the basic structure of a future air wing: two small squadrons of aircraft would serve each of the FP's three groups; and each squadron would dispose of nine aeroplanes making a total of 54. The type of aircraft envisaged were Lockheed Hudsons or Bristol Blenheims, and around 400 air and ground crew would be required to staff the wing. At this stage the question of how to recruit the crew, obtain the aircraft and put in place the necessary infrastructure was not important. What really mattered was convincing Vleeschauwer to give his approval to the project.[2]

Burniaux's plan was to receive a boost through the British Air Training Plan (BCATP), also known as the Empire Air Training Scheme (EATS). Established by the "Riverdale Agreement" of December 1939, the intention of this agreement signed by representatives of Great Britain, Canada, Australia, and New Zealand (named after Arthur Balfour, 1st Baron Riverdale) was to provide training facilities for nearly 50,000 aircrew each year to serve in Commonwealth air forces so as to combat a growing threat from Nazi Germany. Recruits were to receive initial training in their respective countries before receiving advanced training in Canada, while the cost of the training programme was to be shared by the four signatories.[3] In early 1940, the plan was expanded to include South Africa and Southern Rhodesia, and it was to the latter that Burniaux travelled in the hope that Belgian pilots might also receive training. Two other Belgians, Georges Reuter and Désiré Verbraeck, had already enrolled for training with the Rhodesian Air Training Group (RATG) and were receiving training on Oxford and Tiger Moth aircraft at No.21 Flying School in Bulawayo. Subsequently transferred to No.10 Operational Training Unit (OTU) RAF, under the assumed names of Pilot Officer David Carter and John Robinson respectively, Reuter and Verbraeck served with 45 Squadron RAF flying Blenheim Mk.IVF.[4]

An appeal for young men wishing to become aircrew made through Radio Léo on 13 March 1941, and in the daily newspaper *l'Avenir Colonial Belge*, an appeal that generated more than 500 replies,[5] on 22 April 1941 Burniaux obtained permission to travel to Salisbury (Harare) where he hoped to set up an agreement whereby the prospective pilots of the FP's aviation wing could gain training within the RATG. Leaving Léopoldville the following day aboard a Leopard Moth, three days later Burniaux met the then Wing Commander Charles Warburton Meredith. Unable to convince Meredith to accept his proposition, Burniaux turned towards South Africa, where he approached Albert Moulaert, the Belgian Consul

Belgians hopeful of becoming pilots were sent to training schools in South Africa. (Open source)

General in Pretoria. Fortune was on Burniaux's side as it turned out that Moulaert was a close friend of South African General Jan Smuts. Any political obstacle that Burniaux had previously encountered suddenly disappeared and the first contingent of Belgian pilots were due to arrive at 75 Air School at Lyttleton, South Africa in July 1941. Returning to Léopoldville on 15 May 1941, Burniaux then began their selection. Of the 500 who had passed the first stage, 221 candidates were selected for training as pilots. Forming 12 contingents, these men were sent to South Africa between August 1941 and March 1943.[6]

While they were serving members of the FP and served under the authority of the Minister for the Colonies, the selected pilots were seconded to the SAAF for the duration of their training. At its completion, they were then sent to operational squadrons of the SAAF or to RAF squadrons based in the Middle East. With training consisting of three stages – Elementary Flying Training School (EFTS), Service Flying Training School (SFTS) and OTU – similarly to Reuter and Verbraeck before them in Southern Rhodesia most Belgian pilots trained in South Africa were destined to fly light bombers; the type of aircraft FP commanders were intending to use predominantly in the Belgian Congo's future aviation wing. As for Burniaux, he completed training at Bloemfontein and Kimberley on 20 December 1941 and was assigned to the SAAF's 12 Squadron in the Middle East.

Commercial Aviation's Contribution to the FP's Air Wing

Though plans to provide the Belgian Congo with its own military air force were at a standstill, commercial flight was transforming the colony into a hub for international travel due to the avoidance of European air space and the possibility of attack by enemy forces. SABENA had already transferred its operations from Brussels to Marseille during the "Phoney War", and from here it ferried personnel and supplies along the West Africa-Cairo route as well as providing a service to Johannesburg and Cape Town via Elisabethville.[7] Léopoldville's N'Dolo Airfield also serving as a stopover point between southern Europe and South Africa, in March 1941 SABENA moved the remainder of its fleet from Marseille to Léopoldville and established the company's headquarters in the Congolese capital. From Léopoldville, SABENA operated Fokker V-IIs (OO-AIP[8], OO-AIV[9], OO-AIW[10], OO-AIX[11], OO-AIY[12],

Table 14: Civil Aircraft Register – Belgian Congo (aircraft acquired 1934–1944 and registered directly in the Congo)[18]				
Registration	Type	Owners	Date Registered	Fate
OO-CAA	DH.85 Leopard Moth	Robert Auguste Jeanty – Aéroclub du Congo Belge	24/04/1934	Crashed Angola 04/09/1955
OO-CAB	Desouter II	Aéro Club du Katanga	December 1934	Sold 31/10/1936
OO-CAC	DH.80 Puss Moth	Figov	March 1935	Cancelled 14/01/1936
OO-CAD	Caudron C.272/ 5 Luciole	Jean Mathot	23/03/1937	Cancelled 14/08/1944
OO-CAE	Piper J-3 Club		July 1939	Withdrawn from use 04/12/1948
OO-CAF	DH.85 Leopard Moth		June 1940	Cancelled 27/06/1958
OO-CAG	Lockheed 14-H2 Super Electra	Régie Air Afrique/ SABENA	27/09/1940	Sold 25/09/1954
OO-CAH	Lockheed 14-H2 Super Electra	Régie Air Afrique/ SABENA	27/09/1940	Sold 12/07/1947
OO-CAI	Lockheed 18-07 Lodestar	SABENA	03/08/1941	Sold 09/06/1949
OO-CAJ	Lockheed 18-07 Lodestar	SABENA	03/08/1941	Sold 29/10/1948
OO-CAK	Lockheed C-60A Lodestar	SABENA	01/03/1943	Crashed Kenandi 14/01/1945
OO-CAL	Rearwin 8135 Cloudstar		November 1941	
OO-CAM	Rearwin 8135 Cloudstar		November 1941	Cancelled 25/09/1954
OO-CAO	Lockheed C-60A Lodestar	SABENA	05/05/1943	Sold 09/06/1949
OO-CAP	Junkers Ju52 / 3mge	SABENA	February 1942	Withdrawn from use 21/03/1946
OO-CAQ	Piper J-5 Club		November 1942	Reregistered 1961
OO-CAR	Lockheed C-60A Lodestar	SABENA	07/06/1943	Crashed Mitabwa 24/12/1947
OO-CAS	Lockheed C-60A Lodestar	SABENA	07/06/1943	Sold 09/06/1949
OO-CAT	Rearwin 8135 Cloudstar		November 1941	Cancelled 20/02/1946
OO-CAU	Wako YKS-7		July 1943	Crashed 25/09/1954
OO-CAV	Lockheed C-60A Lodestar	SABENA	04/08/1943	Sold 09/06/1949
OO-CAW	Wako YKS-7		June 1944	Cancelled 17/10/1946

OO-AIZ[13]); Caudron C.510 Pelicans (OO-ATF,[14] OO-JHS); Junkers Ju52/3mge (OO-AUF,[15] OO-AUG,[16] OO-AUK)[17]; a DH.80A Puss Moth (OO-EIT); and a DH.85 Leopard Moth (OO-JFC / OO-CAF).

By the end of 1941, SABENA was consolidating its operations and was building accommodation for its staff.

Another important step in the Belgian Congo becoming one of sub-Saharan Africa's largest aviation hubs took place in August

Operated by Pan American Airlines from 1939, the Boeing 314 was powered by four Wright R-2600-3 motors generating 6,400hp and providing a maximum speed of 211mph (340km/h) As for NC-186612, it provided a service across the Atlantic until 1942, the US Navy sold it to American International Airways in 1947. In October of that year, it was sunk at sea by the US Coast Guard for training purposes. *Capetown* the first of 12 Boeing 314s used in the Second World War, Clippers also provided a service between Miami and Léopoldville. British Overseas Airways Corporation also operated 314s. One of its aircraft is pictured here at Léopoldville. (Open source)

This C-60A Lodestar bearing the registration OO-CAV arrived in the Belgian Congo on 4 August 1943 and was sold on 9 June 1949. Operated by SABENA, it was one of three C-60s acquired by the firm. (Belgianwings)

1941 when US President Roosevelt unveiled plans for a commercial airline to be used to transport American Expeditionary Forces (AEF) from West and central Africa to the Middle East. The plan being to use Pointe Noire in the French Congo as a stopover point for travel to Stanleyville and Cairo, the US Civil Aviation Board (CAB) agreed that Pan American Airlines should assure the route. In October another agreement was signed with authorities in the Belgian Congo to create a route linking New York with Léopoldville. Shortly after, in November 1941 Pan Am's "Capetown Clipper" (Boeing 314 Clipper NC-186612) arrived in the Congolese capital having covered some 20,000 miles. This inaugural flight a great success, Pan Am announced that it would begin fortnightly flights from 11 December 1941, just four days after the Japanese attack on Pearl Harbour.

Though agreement had been reached with Free French authorities to use the airfield at Pointe Noire in April 1942, an agreement sealed in exchange for eight Lockheed bombers, French fears that the presence of US aircraft and troops in the French Congo would make the country a target for the Axis led to the US Army displacing the entirety of its operational facilities from Pointe Noire to the Belgian Congolese port of Matadi. These facilities including a hospital and a post office, it also transferred its 38th Engineer Battalion. As part of the 8012 US Army Composite Group, it had built airfields in Senegal, Nigeria, and Morocco. As the centre of US operations had moved to Matadi, its engineers upgraded N'Dolo airfield and extended its runway to a length of 2,300 metres. The US base in the Belgian Congo named after Roosevelt, by mid-September US forces in the colony numbered 1,500.[19]

As N'Dolo gained importance as an air base for Allied operations, as was the case for in the French Congo those in the Belgian Congo were concerned that the colony would come under attack. The Congo's minerals essential to the Allied war effort, in particular uranium deposits used in the Manhattan Project, the Under-Secretary for Defence Henri Rolin made an appeal to British authorities by pointing out that the air defence of the Lower Congo and Matadi was essential. What was needed, in his view, were long-range reconnaissance aircraft to protect coastal areas, and he suggested that this mission could be carried out by the SAAF working alongside those of the Free French. The area of operations of this joint force extending from South Africa to Nigeria, a fighter squadron would be given the role of protecting ports and industries

in the Congo against possible attacks from the Luftwaffe. The overall command of operations handled by the RAF, Rolin also pointed out that the threat of attack came from French colonies under control of the Vichy and situated around the Gulf of Guinea.[20]

Rolin's memorandum submitted to the British Air Ministry on 27 April 1942 but receiving a refusal on the grounds that aircraft were not available, Belgian Prime Minister Hubert Pierlot intervened by contacting Churchill personally. The Air Ministry finally gave in to pressure from Churchill and the British Foreign Office, and on 26 May 1942 it agreed to supply fighter planes but not reconnaissance aircraft. The fighter squadron comprising 24 aircraft was stationed in Léopoldville but fell under the auspices of the West Africa Command (WAC) based in Accra in the Gold Coast and in Nigeria. Performing the functions of an OTU, the squadron in question could provide training to FP officers, but it was not authorised to provide back up for FP operations as would a colonial air force. The choice of aircraft left to the Belgians, Lockheed Lightning P-38s and Curtiss Tomahawk P-40s were put forward as suggestions, but as the P-38 was susceptible to technical problems at the time, the Tomahawk was seen as the best option. The Air Ministry agreeing to Belgian requests, on 24 June 1942 it commandeered 24 of the aircraft that had just been assigned to the RAF's No. 171 Squadron, a unit used for coastal reconnaissance and radio countermeasures. No. 171 then equipped with the P-51 Mustang, the Léopoldville-based unit was identified as No. 349 Squadron. As had been the case with previous efforts to create an air force serving the Belgian Congo this project was also destined to never get off the ground. WAC was not convinced that the Belgian Congo faced any direct threat from Axis powers, and in late October 1942 it decided that No. 349 Squadron was to be based at Ikeja, Nigeria rather than in Léopoldville.[21]

During the summer of 1942, Burniaux returned to Léopoldville as Chief of Staff of the Avimil or Avi / FP (*aviation militaire* or *Aviation militaire Force Publique*). He learnt that the Belgian government was negotiating the return of Belgian pilots serving in the SAAF in the Middle East and had the intention of forcing them to join the RAF Volunteer Reserve (RAFVR). Considering himself as a representative of these pilots, Burniaux expressed his opposition the plan and stated that he had the intention of creating either a flight or a squadron of Belgian aviators that would be seconded to the SAAF. Finally, both the government and Burniaux were to reach a compromise when it was decided that all pilots either having finished their training or still in training would remain with their present units in Southern Rhodesia, Kenya, or Egypt. Fifty-one Belgians concerned by these measures (22 pilots, 13 navigators, none radio operators, and seven technicians), they would then be sent to South Africa and integrated into the SAAF. Most would serve in the Middle East, but some joined transport units, units dealing with maritime surveillance, or operational support units. Seven were awarded the DFC for their actions while seven died in the course of their duty.

Post-War Military Aviation in the Belgian Congo

If the Second World War and the beginning of the Cold War had had taught Belgian military strategists any lessons, it was that threats to the country's existence could emanate from different sources at any given time and in any given place. Challenges to colonial regimes from communist-backed forces only reinforced a feeling of foreboding, and by the beginning of the 1950s the echo of small wars taking place principally in Asia were beginning to rear their head in Africa. The Belgian Congo and other Belgian interests in central Africa were not directly under military threat for the time being, but nonetheless the Belgian government sought reassurance by its starting to consider the Belgian Congo as a smaller version of metropolitan Belgium, and an integral part of its military and financial resources should the Belgian mainland be menaced by the USSR or any other invader. Challenges of a more pacific nature also came through the tenets of the United Nations' founding principles. Its expounding the notion that non-self-governing territories should be granted independence from colonial powers, by arguing that the Belgian Congo was not a colony but a part of Belgium, its government could argue that independence amounted to the illegal division of a sovereign territory. Consequently, Belgium and its overseas possessions should be seen as an organic entity. As such, the national defence of the territory was to be extended to the Belgian Congo.

The first step taken towards organising the defence of Belgian interests in the Congo came in September 1946 and the creation of a mixed military commission, or *Commission militaire mixte* (CMM). Comprising high-ranking officers and representatives of the Belgian government, its role was to study how Belgium's military capacity could be improved in the Congo, after several months of debate in February 1948 the commission reported back to the Belgian Defence Ministry. The report handed in just before the signing of the Western European Union (WEA),[22] it stated that as Belgium had been used as a corridor for previous invasions the Belgian Congo should be used as an auxiliary base for Belgian military operations. Remembering that the Belgian government had to seek exile in London during the First World War and the Second World War, and that relations between Belgian and British authorities had soured in 1944, the report also mentioned that at this point the moving of Belgium's affairs to the Congo had been evoked as a possibility.[23]

The introduction of Belgian metropolitan forces into the Congo changed the face of the colony forever. It put an end to the monopoly the FP had over its protection and was to place the FP under the command of a centralised body responsible for the coordination of military operations in the colony. Known as the *Commandement supérieur des forces métropolitaines d'Afrique* (Cométro) or the High Command for Metropolitan Forces in Africa, this body was based in Léopoldville but received its orders from the Belgian Ministry of Defence.

It was within this context that plans for the construction of a gigantic military base in the heart of central Africa were set in motion. In July 1948 the then Lt. Colonel Emile Janssens was given the mission of finding a suitable area in which the new base could be constructed, and although the land chosen was some 1,200kms from the capital, Kamina in the province of Katanga presented the ideal spot. In proximity to the Congo's main communications arteries and situated on a plateau stretching over some 100 square kms (38 square miles), it was also close to Katanga's mines and mineral resources such as those found at Shinkolobwe, the source of the much sought-after uranium. Constructed between 1949 and 1953 at a cost of 2.5 million Belgian francs, the base was testament to Belgium's commitment to the defence of its colonies and to its will to remain in central Africa for many years to come. With Kamina Air Base codenamed BAKA (*Base Aérienne Katanga*), and two other bases – Bas-Congo (BACO); and Kitona (BAKI) – also serving as military bases, it became Belgium's most strategic base in Africa. Serving as an overseas training base for paracommandos and as a centre for Belgium's *Ecole de Pilotage Avancée* (EPA), or Advanced Training School for Pilots, a variety of different aircraft came to be used for military manoeuvres caried out in the Belgian Congo throughout the 1950s. T-6 Harvards became a prominent feature given the base's status as a pilot training centre, but many other types of carrier and surveillance aircraft were to be transferred from mainland Belgium to the colony or purchased from RAF stocks in Southern Rhodesia. Purchases of aircraft increased towards the completion of BAKA in 1953 and the Mau Mau insurgency in Kenya.

As for the FP's own air wing, the Avimil, its fortunes as an air force replete with a full range of aircraft and worthy of the term 'air force' never completely came to fruition. It looked on in envy at the exploits of the Kenya Police Force (KPR) Reserve Air Wing against the Mau Mau and drew up plans to create a light aircraft wing after one of its pilots, Captain Deschepper attending a training course with the Kenyan unit. The Avimil flying DH. Doves and a DH. Heron purchased from private sources or from SABENA, and with its two Stampe-Vertongens retired from service, Deschepper submitted a report in October 1958 requesting that the FP equip itself with aircraft fit for the creation of a light aircraft squadron. Jansenns approving the acquisition of 12 aircraft in December 1958,[24] the events of January 1959 in the Belgian Congo were to put pay to most plans for the expansion of the Avimil. The unit was, however, to play a significant role in military operations that were to take place throughout the Belgian Congo from that month. (See Chapter 8).

The rifle most prominently used by FP foot soldiers was the Albini or Albini-Braendlin rifle; a Belgian version of the Snider-Enfield breach-loading rifle designed by Italian naval officer Augusto Albini and perfected by English gunsmith Francis Braendlin. (Artwork by Anderson Subtil)

The Maxim machine gun was one of the most powerful weapons of its time, and could fire up to 600 rounds per minute. This recoil-operated machine gun invented by the American-born British inventor Sir Hiram Stevens Maxim in 1884 has been described as the weapon most associated with imperial conquest and the so-called 'Scramble for Africa'. (Artwork by Anderson Subtil)

The 5.7cm Maxim-Nordenfelt *'Canon de caponnière'* was a fortress- and infantry-gun developed in the 1880s in Great Britain, sold to Belgium and later produced under licence by the Cockerill company. It saw much action during the First World War – both in Belgian and German hands. (Artwork by Anderson Subtil)

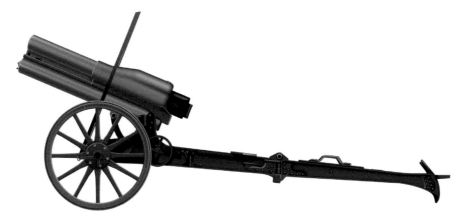

The FP continued to use the 75mm Saint-Chamond gun until the end of the Second World War. A French-made artillery piece, it found use in conflicts as diverse as the Mexican Revolution of 1910–1920, and the 1948 Arab-Israeli War. (Artwork by Anderson Subtil)

Left: the 75mm Krupp Model 1903 field gun could fire shells as well as canister. Used widely by the FP in the First World War, it was produced by German weapons manufacturer Friedrich Krupp AG and continued to see service until the end of the Second World War. Right: the Willys MB became one of the most widely-used and most successful light utility vehicles in the world. Entering production in 1941, vehicles supplied to Belgium through the US Mutual Defence Assistance Programme (MDAP) were to find their way to the Belgian Congo for use by the FP. (Artworks by Anderson Subtil and David Bocquelet)

The GMC CCKW, also known as 'Jimmy', was a cargo truck widely used in the Second World War and the Korean War. In similar fashion to the FP's Willys jeeps, it found its way into the Belgian Congo through the MDAP. (Artwork by David Bocquelet)

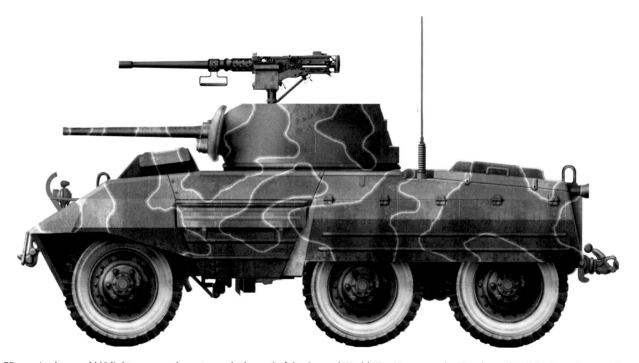

The FP acquired several M8 light armoured cars towards the end of the Second World War. Known as the 'Greyhound' in British service, and first produced in March 1943, the M8 enabled the FP to become fully mobile. (Artwork by David Bocquelet)

The training of the *Force Publique*'s first pilots was carried out using de Havilland DH.82 Tiger Moths of No.21 Flying School in Bulawayo. Training by the Rhodesian Air Training Group (RATG) started in 1940 and was intended to provide pilots and aircrew to serve in Commonwealth forces. (Artwork by Peter Penev)

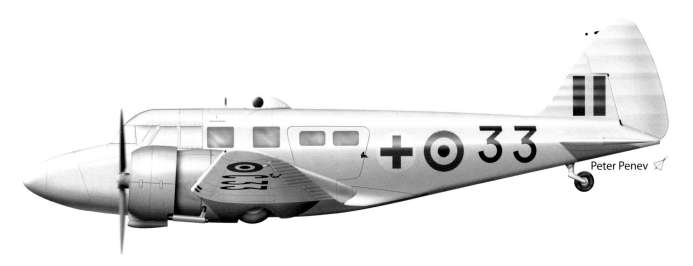

A twin-engined, wooden-frame aircraft, the Airspeed AS.65 Consul was used for communication and casevac. The examples acquired for use in the Belgian Congo had been 'demilitarised' or had been adapted for civilian use. The aircraft was equipped with a wide fright door for casevac missions. Like the majority of the FP's aircraft of the 1930s and 1940s, it was painted in overall high-speed silver finish. (Artwork by Peter Penev)

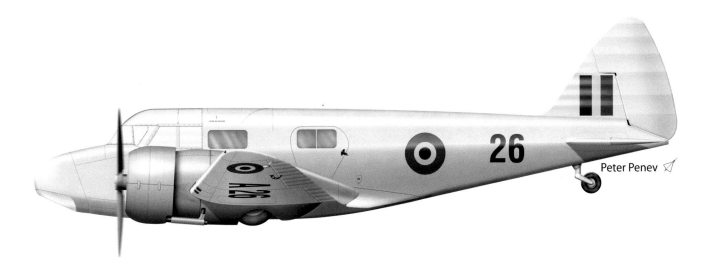

Six Airspeed Oxford C.1 communications aircraft were acquired by the Belgian government in exile for use in the Belgian Congo during the Second World War. Some being used for crop-spraying or for geographical surveys, by 1955 all the FP's Oxfords had been replaced by de Havilland Doves. Wearing the high-speed silver finish overall, they received their full serials applied in black on lower wing surfaces, 'RAF-style'. (Artwork by Peter Penev)

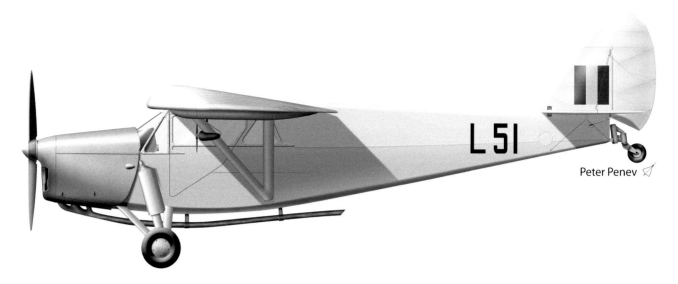

Belgian colonial authorities acquired a de Havilland DH.85 Leopard Moth at the start of the Second World War and acquired two more examples as the war progressed. Used during the East African campaign and serving mainly in Egypt and Sudan, the aircraft were primarily used for communication flights. (Artwork by Peter Penev)

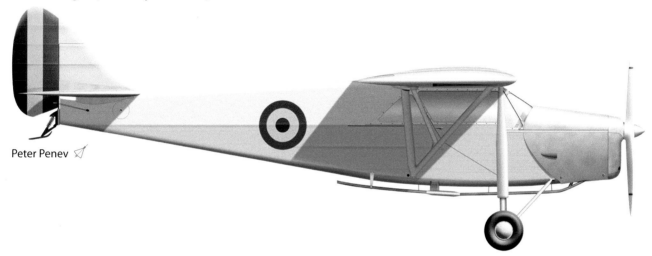

The de Havilland DH.80 Puss Moth was first produced in 1929. Mainly used as private aircraft, in the Belgian Congo it was operated by the airline SABENA and for liaison purposes. As usual for the 1930s and 1940s, Belgian Puss Moths were usually painted in high-speed silver finish overall, except for the engine cowling, which was left in bare metal overall. (Artwork by Peter Penev)

During the East Africa Campaign, the RAF assigned a Hawker Hardy from No. 237 Squadron (Southern Rhodesia) to assist the Belgian colonial authorities. Starting its service with *the Force Publique* on 14 May 1941, the aircraft landed heavily during a rainstorm at Gambela in Ethiopia and was destroyed. As far as is known, it wore a camouflage pattern in dark brown and dark green on upper surfaces and sides, while undersides were painted in light grey. (Artwork by Peter Penev)

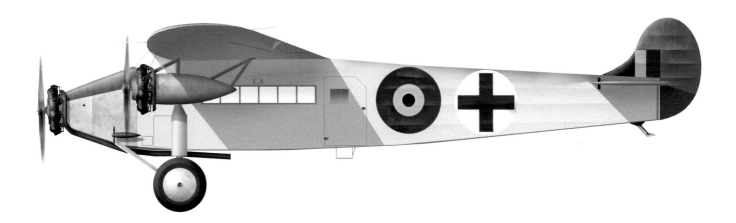

A Fokker F.VII operated by SABENA was still at the forefront of its operations from early 1935, even if gradually phased out in favour of the faster Savoia-Marchetti S.73 from October 1936. A least two of SABENA's F.VII were requisitioned by the FP for use as casevac aircraft during the Kenya campaign in the Second World War. (Artwork by Tom Cooper)

Another aircraft acquired by SABENA to replace the Fokker F.VII was the Junkers Ju-52M-3. At least three were used by the FP to support troops in Ethiopia during the East Africa campaign while others served as ferry aircraft between Egypt and central Africa. (Artwork by Peter Penev)

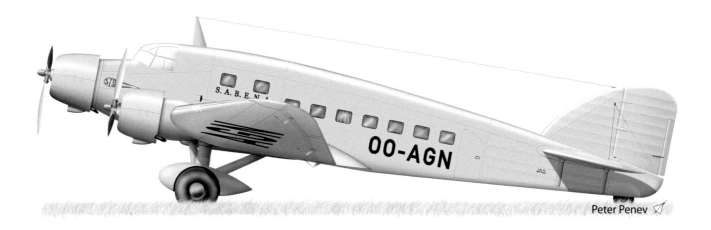

SABENA's remaining fleet of seven SM.73s were requisitioned by Belgian authorities in May 1940. Taken to Great Britain, the aircraft were to be used for the training of Belgian pilots but finished their journey in Algiers and under the control of the Vichy government. Though the aircraft were acquired by the Belgian government and flown by Belgian pilots before their arrival in Algeria, they were never officially incorporated into the FP. (Artwork by Peter Penev)

In addition to wearing the old blue serge uniform of a *Force Publique* Askari, this native bugler from around 1885 is shown with a red fez on his head, which would become the main visual mark of this service. The leatherwork is probably a simplified version of the Belgian Royal Army equipment from this period. While not shown in this artwork, the primary firearm of the *Force Publique* in this period was the 11mm M1873 Albini rifle. (Artwork by Anderson Subtil)

Although there is some uncertainty, the uniform illustrated here from 1916 seems to have belonged to an intermediate design, made of khaki-grey material, with a light edging on the collar and running down the edges of the chest opening. The old, leather ammunition pouches gave way for modern British Mills webbing, better suited for rifle magazines. Notable is the khaki overlay on the fez and the introduction of gaiters, although the natives remained barefoot. The firearm of the time was the Belgian Model 1889 rifle, based on the Mauser design, and with M1916 bayonet attached. (Artwork by Anderson Subtil)

By 1940, the *Force Publique* was issued uniforms very similar to those of other colonial troops in Africa, including shorts and rank markings on the sleeves of the tunic. The fez (tarbush) had a canvas neck protector attached and, on the front, the metallic emblem of the FP. Combat gear was carried in a canvas rucksack or strapped to the 1937 Pattern Web Equipment. Notable were a canteen of British issue and a manchette and that, unlike earlier troops, this corporal wore reinforced leather sandals. His bolt-action rifle was a 7.65x53mm M1935 Belgian Mauser rifle. (Artwork by Anderson Subtil)

A North American T-6 Texan – serial number H216 – in flight over the Belgian Congo in the early 1950s. (Daniel Brackx Collection, via author)

Gaudily painted in bright yellow overall, this piper Cub of the FP – serial P61 – was photographed in 1959 or 1960. (via Piere Gillard)

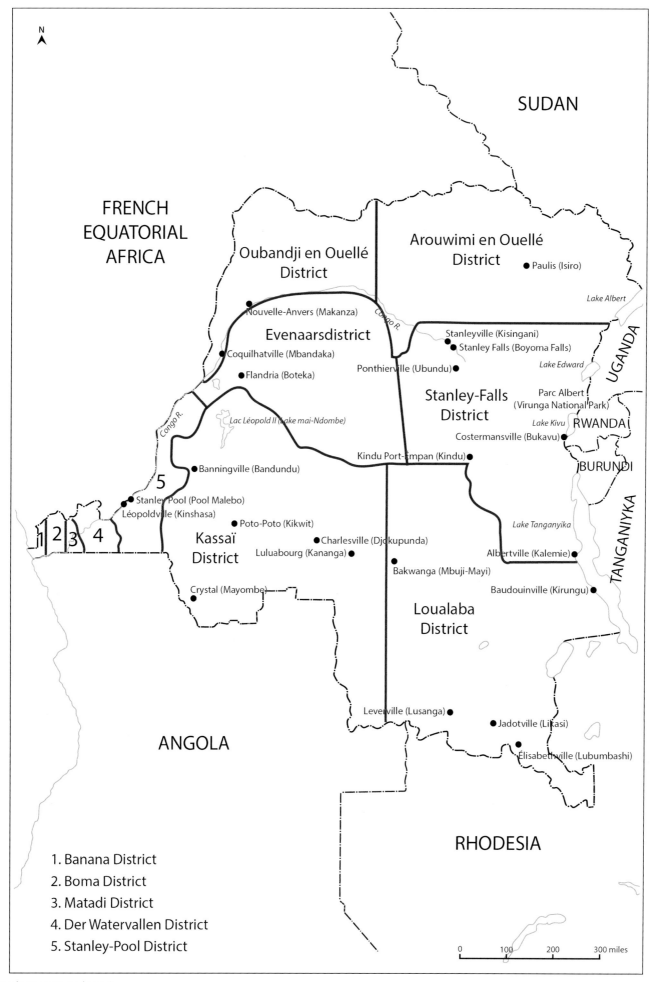

N

SUDAN

FRENCH
EQUATORIAL
AFRICA

Oubandji en Ouellé
District

Arouwimi en Ouellé
District

● Paulis (Isiro)

Lake Albert

● Nouvelle-Anvers (Makanza)

Congo R.

Evenaarsdistrict

● Coquilhatville (Mbandaka)

● Stanleyville (Kisingani)
● Stanley Falls (Boyoma Falls)

Ponthierville (Ubundu) ●

Lake Edward

UGANDA

● Flandria (Boteka)

Congo R.

Lac Léopold II (Lake mai-Ndombe)

Stanley-Falls
District

Parc Albert
(Virunga National Park)

Lake Kivu RWANDA

Costermansville (Bukavu) ●

Kindu Port-Empan (Kindu) ●

BURUNDI

5

● Banningville (Bandundu)

● Stanley Pool (Pool Malebo)
Léopoldville (Kinshasa)

Kassaï
District

● Poto-Poto (Kikwit)

● Charlesville (Djokupunda)
Luluabourg (Kananga) ●

Lake Tanganyika

TANGANIYKA

Albertville (Kalemie) ●

Bakwanga (Mbuji-Mayi) ●

Baudouinville (Kirungu) ●

● Crystal (Mayombe)

Loualaba
District

1 2 3 4

Leverville (Lusanga) ●

Jadotville (Likasi) ●

ANGOLA

Élisabethville (Lubumbashi) ●

RHODESIA

1. Banana District
2. Boma District
3. Matadi District
4. Der Watervallen District
5. Stanley-Pool District

0   100   200   300 miles

(Map by George Anderson)

AIRCRAFT USED BY THE AVIMIL OR THE BAF IN THE BELGIAN CONGO

AIRSPEED AS.10 OXFORD C.1

A twin-engined, wooden-frame aircraft used for evasan (casualty evacuation) and made by Airspeed Ltd of the United Kingdom. With 4,411 examples produced between 1937–1945, the AS.10 was intended for advanced pilot training, navigation training, as well as training linked to photographic observation, bombing and radio communications. Six Oxfords were acquired by the Belgian government in exile from the British Air Ministry in the Second World War for use by the FP in the Belgian Congo. In 1955, all Oxfords were replaced by DH Doves.[25] One Oxford crashed at Luanda during an official visit in the Second World War, while another made a forced landing in Cabinda and was used henceforth by Portuguese authorities in Angola.

Table 15: Airspeed AS.10 Oxford C.1			
Registration[26]	Date in	Date out	Service record
LX528 (RAF)	June 1944	1955	A-21, N'Dolo then the technical college for the training of mechanics at Kamina Air Base (BAKA)
NM447 (RAF)	June 1944	1955	A-22
NM450 (RAF)	June 1944	1955	A-23, adapted in 1948 for crop spraying
NM464 (RAF)	June 1944	1955	A-24
NM466 (RAF)	June 1944	1955	A-25, adapted in 1948 for crop spraying
NM467 (RAF)	June 1944	1955	A-26, used for aerial observation and geographical survey

A-21 was transferred to the BAF's Air Training School at BAKA. (Daniel Brackx)

A-23 of the FP is assembled at Léopoldville in 1944. (Daniel Brackx)

A-24 (possibly) is assembled at Léopoldville in 1944. (Jean-Louis Roba Collection courtesy of Belgianwings)

A-26 at BAKA. (Jacques Schelfaut Collection courtesy of Belgianwings)

AIRSPEED AS.65 CONSUL

A twin-engined, wooden-frame aircraft used for communication and casevac. Produced by Airspeed between 1946–1958, the examples acquired for the Belgian Congo had been "demilitarised" or adapted for passenger transport (four or five passengers). Equipped with a wide freight door allowing for casevac operations.

Registration[27]	c/n	Date in	Date out	Service record
Table 16: Airspeed AS.65 Consul				
C-31	5190	1948	August 1955	Acquired by Natal Airlines (ZS-DNJ), crashed at Matatiele, South Africa, 8 May 1956
C-32	5178	December 1948	August 1955	Ex G-AKCV, then ZS-DNM. Crashed Luluaburg 1951
C-33	5189	December 1948	August 1955	Acquired by Natal Airlines (ZS-DNK), dismantled September 1959
C-34	5133	March 1949	August 1955	Ex G-AJLO, then Natal Airlines (ZS-DNL), dismantled in October 1958
C-35	5191	1949	1954	Crashed at Léopoldville, cancelled
C-36	5193	1949	1955	Cancelled

C-31 is refuelled in the Belgian Congo. (Daniel Brackx)

C-32 in flight over the Belgian Congo between 1948–1955. (Leif Hellström Collection courtesy of Belgianwings)

C-34 undergoing maintenance at N'Dolo air base, Léopoldville. (Jean Michotte Collection courtesy of Belgianwings)

C-36 undergoing maintenance at N'Dolo air base, Léopoldville. (Daniel Brackx)

BRISTOL 171 SYCAMORE HR.14B

Built by a division of the Bristol Aeroplane Company in the UK and making its first flight in July 1947, the Bristol Sycamore has the distinction of becoming the first British-designed helicopter to be used by the RAF. Performing six main roles (search and rescue, air ambulance, passenger transport, freight transport, aerial crane and dual instruction), the Sycamore saw service in the Malayan Emergency, the Cyprus Emergency and the Aden Emergency. As for the Belgian Congo, three Sycamores were purchased from the RAF in 1954 to operate out of BAKA.

Table 17: Bristol 171 Sycamore HR.14B				
Registration[28]	c/n	Date in	Date out	Service record
B-1	13199	June 1954	March 1960	G-AMWP, B-1 / OT-ZKA, crashed Lumwe, March 1960.
B-2	13200	June 1954	August 1960	G-AMWR, B-2 / OT-ZKB, destroyed on arrival of UN troops at BAKA.
B-3	13201	June 1954	July 1960	G-AMWS, B-3 / OT-ZKC, crashed Busangu July 1960.

Bristol Sycamore registration B-2 at BAKA. Designed by the Bristol Aeroplane Company in the UK, the Sycamore saw service in a number of colonial conflicts fought by the British. (Daniel Brackx)

Bristol Sycamore registration B-3 was destroyed by UNOC troops at Kamina in August 1960. (Daniel Brackx)

CAUDRON C.282 / 8 SUPER PHALÈNE
A single-engine, four-seat aircraft with a wooden and steel frame, plywood and canvas covering. Produced by Avions Caudron SA France between 1932–1939.

Table 18: Caudron C.282 / 8 Super Phalène				
Registration	c/n	Date in	Date out	Service record
	6764-16	1940	25/04/1940	Registered as OO-ATI in 1936. Requisitioned by the FP from private ownership in 1940 for use in local operations. Crashed 25/04/1940.[29]

Members of the *Force Publique* in front of Caudron C.282 / 8 Super Phalène. (Daniel Brackx)

Caudron C.510 Pélican

A single-engine, four-seat aircraft with a wooden and steel frame, plywood and canvas covering. Produced by Avions Caudron SA France between 1932–1939.

Table 19: Caudron C.510 Pélican				
Registration	c/n	Date in	Date out	Service record
C-22	7664/56	6/11/1940	22/10/1945	Requisitioned by the FP on 6/11/1940, OO-ATF was based in Watsa and was used in operations around the Sudan- Ethiopia border. Made forced landing between Khartoum and Malakal 1/04/1941[30]

Nicknamed "Bolikoko", OO-ATF wore the colours of the *Force Publique* during its service in the Second World War. (Daniel Brackx)

DE HAVILLAND DH.60G GIPSY MOTH

A single-engine, two-seat biplane with a plywood and canvas covering. Produced by de Havilland Aircraft Company, UK, and requisitioned from private ownership and used for liaison and reconnaissance.

Registration	c/n	Date in	Date out	Service record
Table 20: De Havilland DH.60G Gipsy Moth				
C-23	1875	26/10/1940	December 1943	Operated between Banana and Moanda and used for target practice by anti-aircraft defences at Matadi. Flew with Belgian colours.[31]

DE HAVILLAND DH.80A PUSS MOTH

A three-engine, three-seat aircraft with a structure composed of metal tubing, plywood and canvas covering. Produced by de Havilland between 1929–1933.

Registration	c/n	Date in	Date out	Service record
Table 21: De Havilland DH.80A Puss Moth				
	2210	February 1941 (November 1940 according to another source).[32]	01/12/1943	Operated from Watsa and used around the Sudan-Ethiopia border. Flew Belgian colours.[33] Cancelled 04/08/1945.

Members of the *Force Publique* pictured next to OO-AMN. (Daniel Brackx)

DE HAVILLAND DH.85 LEOPARD MOTH

Single-engine, three-seat, high-wing monoplane produced by de Havilland between 1933 – 1936. The successor to the Puss Moth and the first aircraft used by the FP.

Registration	c/n	Date in	Date out	Service record
Table 22: De Havilland DH.85 Leopard Moth				
C-1 / L-51	7092	09/10/1940	25/09/1954	OO-AVD (1935), OO-CAF (1940), C-1, L-51. Based at N'Dolo, it was cancelled 27/06/1958 after a crash at Boma.
	7038	26/10/1940	01/12/1943	G-ACOS, OO-BOB, OO-CAA (1934). Crashed Angola 04/09/1955, cancelled 12/09/1955.

C-1 was acquired by Belgian colonial authorities in October 1940 for use by the *Force Publique*. It was used in conjunction with OO-ATF and OO-AMN along the Sudan/Ethiopia border during the East Africa Campaign. (Daniel Brackx)

The first aircraft acquired for use by the *Force Publique*, the same aircraft is pictured undergoing maintenance at N'Dolo. (Jean Michotte Collection courtesy of Belgianwings)

DE HAVILLAND DH.104 DOVE34

A single-engine, short-haul airliner produced by de Havilland between 1946 – 1967.

Table 23: De Havilland DH.104 Dove					
Registration	Type	c/n	Date In	Date Out	Identification
D-10	Dove 2	04252	August 1954	April 1957	OO-CGG
D-11	Dove 2	04080	October 1949	July 1960	OT-CFK
D-12	Dove 1B	04054	June 1950	October 1958	
D-14	Dove 1B	04367	November 1952	July 1960	OT-CFM
D-15	Dove 1B	04442	October 1953	July 1960	OT-CFN
D-16	Dove 1B	04443	November 1953	July 1960	OT-CFP
D-17	Dove 1B	04447	February 1954	July 1960	OT-CFQ
D-18	Dove 1B	04154	July 1952	July 1960	OT-CFR
D-19	Dove 1B	04013	May 1956	July 1960	OT-CFS
D-20	Dove 1/5	04013	May 1956	July 1960	OT-CFT
D-21	Dove 5	04506	November 1959	July 1960	
D-22	Dove 5	04507	November 1959	July 1960	

Registration	Service record
D-10	Crashed N'Dolo Airfield, date unknown.
D-11	D-11, then KAT-11 (FAK), it was destroyed at Ngule by a Saab J29 Tunnan of the UN on 12 December 1961.
D-12	Crashed near Nialamgira, date unknown.
D-14	D-14, then KAT-14 (FAK). Captured and vandalised by United Nations Operations Congo (UNOC) troops at Elisabethville on 28 August 1961.
D-15	D-15, then KAT-15 (FAK), it became 9Q-COB (Congolese Government) in 1964. From then, 9T-DGA of *Force Aérienne Congolaise* (FAC). Piloted by Jean-Claude Gengler and co-piloted by Jean Massart, it crashed at Ndjili in 1965.
D-16	D-16, then FAC 9T-P40.
D-17	D-17, then KAT-17 (FAK). Captured by UNOC troops 28 August 1961 at Elisabethville or Usumbura and transferred to FAC 9T-P41 in 1963.
D-18	VP-YHV of Central African Airways until 1948, then D-18, then KAT-18. Captured and vandalised by UNOC troops Elisabethville 28 August 1961.
D-19	OO-AWE until 1956, then D-19, then KAT-19, then FAC 9T-P42 1963.
D-20	D-20, then KAT-20 (FAK), destroyed in a crash at Manono 31 January 1961.
D-21	Vandalised July 1960, then transferred to FAC 9T-P43.
D-22	D-22, then KAT-22 (FAK) and KA-T22 (FAK), flown to Angola 27 January 1963 and scrapped.

D-12 is watched over by a soldier of the *Force Publique* at BAKA. (Jacques Schelfaut Collection courtesy of Belgianwings)

D-14 in flight over the Belgian Congo. (Daniel Brackx)

D-16 in flight over one of the Congo's numerous lakes. (Guy Destrebecq Collection courtesy of Belgianwings)

D-22 during its time with the Force Aérienne Katangaise. (Daniel Brackx)

DE HAVILLAND DH.114 HERON 2

A four-engine, propeller-driven liaison airliner built by De Haviland. A development of the DH.104 Dove, 149 were built from 1950.

Table 24: De Havilland DH.114 Heron 2				
Registration	c/n	Date in	Date out	Service record
OO6CGG	14055	25 May 1954	July 1960	G-ANPV, then OO-CGG, DI, 90-OCG, OT-CFZ, and KAT-01. Captured and vandalised by UNOC troops at Elisabethville, 28 August 1961.

Obtained by Belgian colonial authorities for use by the Governor General of the Belgian Congo, OO-CGG (Governor General) was then used by Katangese premier Moïse Tshombe after the independence of the Congo and the secession of Katanga in July 1960. (Daniel Brackx)

DOUGLAS C-47B SKYTRAIN / DAKOTA IV

Developed from the DC-3 civilian airliner, the Skytrain was used extensively by the Allies in the Second World War as a troop and cargo carrier. Produced from 1941 by the Douglas Aircraft Company in the United States. When in use by British and Commonwealth forces, the Skytrain was referred to as the 'Dakota'. This is possibly from the acronym "DACoTA" for Douglas Aircraft Company Transport Aircraft. As for the Belgian Congo, the creation of a transport wing was seen as a priority after the Second World War. Many Dakotas were purchased through America's Foreign Liquidation Commission (FLC), the plan to liquidate surplus military material left in Europe by US forces (1946–1947). Over the coming years, several of the examples purchased were to be based in the Belgian Congo.

Table 25: Douglas C-47B Skytrain / Dakota IV				
Registration	c/n	Date in	Date out	Service record
K-1	15056/26501	December 1953	14/01/1954	43-49240 (USAAF) 1944, OO-SMA 1952 (SABENA), K-1, temporarily used by FP.
K-02	20741	August 1946	13/09/1953	43-16275 (USAAF) 1944. K-2, KP-2. Temporarily used by FP. Forced landing near Kolwezi, not repaired, fuselage used for training by paratroopers at Kolwezi.
K-06	20884	August 1946	June 1957	43-16418 (USAAF), K-6/OT-CWC, KP-6/OT-CNW, crashed during take-off Albertville 9 June 1957.
K-18	14603/26048	February 1947	December 1958	43-18787 (USAAF), K-18/OT-CWH, crashed Paulis (now Isiro) 01/12/1958.
K-19	15809/32557	January 1950	February 1961	44-76225 (USAAF), K-19/OT-CWI, K-19, KAT-03, destroyed.
K-21	15810/32558	July 1947	February 1961	44-76226 (USAAF), KN305 (RAF), K-21/OT-CWJ, KAT-02 (FAK), destroyed 25/04/1961.

Dakota IV				
Registration	c/n	Date in	Date out	Service record
K-40	16496/33244	May 1953		44-76912 (USAAF) 1944, KN601 (RAF) 1945, K-40, temporarily used by FP.

After making a forced landing at Lualaba in 1953, K-2/KP-2 was used to train paratroopers at Kolwezi. (Daniel Brackx)

K-18 sits on the runway at Melsbroek, Belgium. Behind is a Pan American Airways Boeing 377 Stratocruiser. (Air Historical Team KLM/MRA courtesy of Belgianwings)

K-19 pictured at Stanleyville in the late 1950s. Alongside K-19 is a Harvard III AT-6D (H-38) (R. Clarisse courtesy of Belgianwings)

FOKKER F.VII/3M

A two-seat, transport aircraft capable of carrying 10 passengers with a frame made from metal tubing and covered in canvas and plywood. Manufactured in the Netherlands by NV Koninklijke Nederlandse Vliegtuigenfabriek Fokker from 1924, two of SABENA's F. VIIs were requisitioned to serve as medical aircraft during the British military campaign in Kenya in the Second World War.

Table 26: Fokker F.VII/3m				
Registration	c/n	Date in	Date out	Service record
-	-	01/12/1940	September 1941	OO-AIV (SABENA), cancelled 6 August 1945
-	-	October 1941	June 1942	OO-AIX (SABENA), cancelled 6 August 1945.

HAWKER HARDY

A two-seat biplane, the Hawker Hardy was a general-purpose variant of the Hawker Hart.

Table 27: Hawker Hardy				
Registration	c/n	Date in	Date out	Service record
K4316	-	14/05/1941	26/05/1941	K4316 (SAAF), Belgian colonial authorities bought the aircraft from the SAAF. Wearing Belgian colours, it crashed just 12 days later at Gambela in Ethiopia.

The *Force Publique*'s Caudron C.510 Pélican temporarily grounded, to provide air power during the East Africa Campaign the RAF assigned a Hawker Hardy from N°237 Squadron (Southern Rhodesia) to assist the Belgian colonial authorities. Starting its service with the *Force Publique* on 14 May 1941, the aircraft landed heavily during a rainstorm at Gambela in Ethiopia and was destroyed. (Jean-Louis Roba Collection courtesy of Belgianwings)

JUNKERS JU 52/ 3MGE

A three-engine transport aircraft with capacity for 16 passengers or 12 stretchers. Requisitioned from SABENA for use by the Belgian Congo military authorities as a passer and cargo carrier during the FP's Ethiopia campaign. According to one source, at least three Junkers were used by the *Force Publique* on a regular basis.[35]

Table 28: Junkers Ju 52/ 3mge				
Registration	c/n	Date in	Date out	Service record
OO-AGU	-	08/05/1941	06/07/1942	OO-AGU (SABENA) 1939, fate unknown.
OO-AUF	6410	8/05/1941	6/07/1942	OO-AUF (SABENA) 1939. Crashed Mongena, South Africa, 03/04/1944, cancelled 13/02/1948
OO-AUK	5852	8/05/1941	6/07/1942	OO-AUK (SABENA) 1939, cancelled 22/11/1946, sold to Transport Aérien du Gabon

NORTH AMERICAN HARVARD/TEXANS (KNOWN TO HAVE SEEN SERVICE IN THE BELGIAN CONGO)

Manufactured by North American Aviation, the T-6 Texan was a trainer aircraft that could be adapted to a combat role. Known as the T-6 Harvard outside of the United States, the T-6 saw service in the Second World War, the Korean War, the Vietnam War as well as several colonial wars. As for T-6s used in the Belgian Congo, it will be noted that almost all the examples listed below had seen service with the RAF and SAAF before service in the Congo. In 1953, 24 former RAF Harvard IIs were transferred from Bulawayo in Southern Rhodesia earning the aircraft the sobriquet "Bulawayos". These aircraft based at Kamina Air Base, they remained unarmed until 1959 when serious demonstrations wracked the Congo. Used as a training tool for Belgian pilots having completed initial training at the BAF's Elementary Flying School at Goetsenhoven, Belgium, in 1959, 16 examples were armed with two 7.62mm machineguns, two Alcan 261 bomb racks and two Matra 13 rocket launchers. Designated 4KA (A meaning "armed"), these aircraft formed units known as *Flight Appui Feu* (FAF), or Fire Assistance Flights.[36] Notably, they served during Operation Mangrove of July 1960, an operation covered in a subsequent chapter.

Table 29: North American Harvard / Texan					
Registration	c/n	Type	Date in	Date out	Service record
H-002	88-15054	III/6D	February 1947	August 1958	41-33947 (USAAF), EX974 (RAF), 7531 (SAAF), EX974 (RAF), H-2, scrapped at Kamina.
H-005	88-14882	III/6D	February 1947	January 1958	41-33910 (USAAF), EX937 (RAF), 7493 (SAAF), EX937 (RAF), H-5, scrapped at Kamina.
H-007	88-15690	III/6D	February 1947	August 1958	41-34059 (USAAF), EZ186 (RAF), 7563 (SAAF), EZ186 (RAF), H-7, scrapped at Kamina.
H-017	88-10635	IIa/6C	April 1947	May 1958	41-33515 (USAAF), EX542 (RAF), 7269 (SAAF), EX542 (RAF), H-17, OO-GEM (Cogea Nouvelle), WE-2 (?), FAC.
H-018	88-9260	IIa/6C	March 1947	May 1958	41-33154 (USAAF), EX181 (RAF), 7045 (SAAF), EX181 (RAF), H-18, OO-GEQ (Cogea Nouvelle), KA-26 (FAK).
H-022	88-9670	IIa/6D/4KA	March 1947	August 1962	41-33237 (USAAF), EX264 (RAF), 7107 (SAAF), EX264 (RAF), H-22 4KA, H-22 (FAC), 9T-P31 (FAC).
H-023	88-16076	III/6D/4KA	March 1947	August 1962	42-84295 (USAAF), EZ292 (RAF), 7622(SAAF), EZ292 (RAF), H-23 4KA, H-23 (FAC), 9T-P? (FAC)

Table 29: North American Harvard / Texan (*continued*)

H-026	88-10014	IIa/6C	June 1947	May 1958	41-33344 (USAAF), EX371 (RAF), 7187 (SAAF), H-26, OO6GEN (Cogea Nouvelle), KA-28 (FAK).
H-028	88-10554	IIa/6C	March 1947	May 1958	41-33434 (USAAF), EX461 (RAF), 7210 (SAAF), EX461 (RAF), H-28, OO-GEO (Cogea Nouvelle), KA-33 (FAK).
H-031	88-12327	IIa/6C	March 1947	August 1958	41-33634 (USAAF), EX661 (RAF), 7315, EX661 (RAF), H-31, OO-GER (Cogea Nouvelle), KA-30 (FAK).
H-034	88-14717	III/6D/4KA	March 1947	August 1958	41-33883 (USAAF), EX910 (RAF), 7476 (SAAF), EX910 (RAF), H-34 4KA, 9T-P? (FAC).
H-035	88-14884	III/6D/4KA	March 1947	August 1958	41-33912 (USAAF), EX939 (RAF), 7505 (SAAF), EX99 (RAF), H-35 4KA, 9T-P35 (FAC).
H-036	88-9869	IIa/6C	March 1947	August 1958	41-332246 (USAAF), EX273 (RAF), 7184 (SAAF), H-36, OO-GES (Cogea Nouvelle), KA-27 (FAK).
H-037	88-9778	IIa/6C	April 1947	August 1958	41-33278 (USAAF), EX305 (RAF), 7115 (SAAF), EX305 (RAF), H-37, OO-GDK (Cogea Nouvelle), 9T-P47 (FAC).
H-038	88-14936	III/6D	May 1947	January 1958	41-33919 (USAAF), EX946 (RAF), 7501 (SAAF), EX946 (RAF), H-.8, scrapped at Kamina.
H-042	88-12067	IIa/6C	March 1947	August 1958	41-33596 (USAAF), EX623 (RAF), 7344 (SAAF), EX623 (RAF), H-42, OO-GDL (Cogea Nouvelle), KA-29 (FAK).
H-043	88-13598	IIa/6C	March 1947	August 1958	41-33752 (USAAF), EX779 (RAF), 7409 (SAAF), EX779 (RAF), H-43, OO-GDM (Cogea Nouvelle), KA-25 (FAK).
H-044	88-16151	III/6D	May 1947	August 1958	42-84370 (USAAF), EZ307 (RAF), 7623 (SAAF), H-34, scrapped at Kamina.
H-045	88-12546	IIa/6C	May 1947	May 1958	41-33653 (USAAF), EX680 (RAF), 7329 (SAAF), EX680 (RAF), H-45, OO-GEP (Cogea Nouvelle), WE-2? (FAC).
H-048	78-6562	IIa/6A		August 1958	41-16184 (USAAF), NC55725, H-48, OO-GDN (Cogea Nouvelle), KA-34 (FAK).
H-052	14A-1909	IIIb	September 1949	August 1958	KF415 'FG', FAD: A (RAF), OO-GDO (Cogea Nouvelle), KA-32 (FAK).
H-102	121-41988	III/6D	June 1950	August 1958	44-81266 (USAAF), H-60 (BLu), H-102, withdrawn from use Kamina.
H-105	88-15448	III/6D	June 1950	August 1958	42-34214 (USAAF), H-63 (BLu), H-105, withdrawn from use Kamina.
H-107	88-16089	III/6D	December 1950	August 1958	42-84308 (USAAF), H-107, withdrawn from use Kamina.
H-108	88-17156	III/6D/4K	December 1950	1961	42-85365 (USAAF), H-108, part of Nossin display team, withdrawn from use Kamina.
H-109	121-41606	III/6D/4K	December 1950	1961	44-80844 (USAAF), H-109, part of Nossin display team, withdrawn from use Kamina.
H-110	121-42271	III/6D/4K	December 1950	August 1958	44-81549 (USAAF), H-110, used as instructional airframe, withdrawn from use Kamina.
H-111	88-14907	III/6D/4K	February 1951	1960	42-44643 (USAAF), H-111, part of Nossin display team, abandoned Kamina.
H-112	88-16735	III/6D	February 1951	1961	42-84954 (USAAF), H-112, withdrawn from use Kamina.
H-113	88-17846	III/6D	February 1951	August 1952	42-86056 (USAAF), H-113, crashed Laminne, 24/06/1952.
H-114	121-42010	III/6D	February 1951	August 1958	44-81288 (USAAF), H-114, withdrawn from use Kamina.
H-115	121-42090	III/6D	February 1951	November 1957	44-81368 (USAAF), H-115, crashed Lake Kyungu, 14/02/1957.

Table 29: North American Harvard / Texan (*continued*)

H-117	CCF4-327	III/6D/4KA	September 1953	December 1959	51-17145 (USAAF), H-117, withdrawn from use Kamina.
H-118	CCF4-326	4/4K	September 1953	November 1959	51-17144 (USAAF), H-118, withdrawn from use Kamina.
H-119	CCF4-330	4	September 1953	March 1954	51-17148 (USAAF), H-119, crashed Kamina, 26/01/1954.
H-120	CCF4-331	4	September 1953	November 1958	51-17149 (USAAF), crashed Kilombo, 31/08/1956.
H-121	CCF4-347	4/4K	September 1953	October 1959	51-17165 (USAAF), H-122, withdrawn from service Kamina.
H-122	CCF4-324	4/4K	September 1953	October 1959	51-17142 (USAAF), H-122, withdrawn from use Kamina.
H-123	CCF4-329	4/4K	September 1953	March 1960	51-17147 (USAAF), H-123, withdrawn from use Kamina.
H-124	CCF4-332	4/4K	September 1953	October 1959	51-17150 (USAAF), H-124, withdrawn from use Kamina.
H-125	CCF4-151	4/4K	October 1950	January 1960	51-17169 (USAAF), destroyed 23/12/1959 when hit by H-136 at Kamina.
H-126	CCF4-352	4/4K	October 1953	March 1960	51-17170 (USAAF), H-126, withdrawn from use Kamina.
H-127	CCF4-353	4	October 1953	August 1955	51-17171 (USAAF), H-127, withdrawn from use Kamina.
H-128	CCF4-354	4	October 1953	August 1955	51-17172 (USAAF), H-128, withdrawn from use Kamina.
H-129	CCF4-362	4	October 1953	January 1958	51-17180 (USSAAF), H-129, unknown.
H-130	CCF4-363	4/4K	October 1953	March 1960	51-17181 (USAAF), H-130, withdrawn from use Kamina.
H-131	CCF4-364	4/4K	October 1953	March 1960	51-17182 (USAAF), H-130, withdrawn from use Kamina.
H-132	CCF4-367	4/4K	October 1953	March 1960	51-17185 (USAAF), H-130, withdrawn from use Kamina
H-133	CCF4-393	4	November 1953	June 1954	51-17211 (USAAF), H-113, crashed 25 km from Kamina, 08/04/1954.
H-134	CCF4-382	4/4K	November 1953	March 1960	51-17200 (USAAF), H-134, withdrawn from use Kamina.
H-135	CCF4-277	4/4K	November 1953	1961	51-17095 (USAAF), H-135, withdrawn from use Kamina.
H-136	CCF4-381	4/4K	November 1953	January 1960	51-17199 (USAAF), H-136, destroyed when crashing into H-125, Kamina, 23/12/1959.
H-137	CCF4-365	4/4K	October 1953	1961	51-17183 (USAAF), H-137, withdrawn from use Kamina.
H-138	CCF4-391	4/4K	October 1953	1961	51-17209 (USAAF), H-138, withdrawn from use Kamina.
H-139	CCF4-378	4/4K	October 1953	1961	51-17196 (USAAF), H-139, withdrawn from use Kamina.
H-140	CCF4-392	4	November 1953	October 1955	51-17210 (USAAF), H-140, crashed Kamina, 08/09/1955.
H-141	CCF4-399	4/4K	November 1953	1961	51-17217 (USAAF), H-141, withdrawn from use Kamina
H-142	CCF4-396	4/4K	November 1953	July 1960	51-17214, H-142, destroyed when landing at Kamina, 29/04/1960.
H-143	CCF4-398	4/4K	November 1953	1961	51-17216 (USAAF), H-143, withdrawn from use Kamina.
H-144	CCF4-397	4/4K	November 1953	1961	51-17215 (USAAF), H-144, withdrawn from use Kamina.

Table 29: North American Harvard / Texan (*continued*)					
H-145	CCF4-311	4/4K	November 1953	1961	51-17129 (USAAF), H-145, withdrawn from use Kamina.
H-146	CCD4-323	4/4K	November 1953	1961	51-17141 (USAAF), H-146, withdrawn from use Kamina.
H-201	88-10249	IIa/6C	January 1954	July 1956	41-22292 (USAAF), EC419, H.87 (RAF), H-201 withdrawn from use Kamina.
H-202	88-10627	IIa/6C/4KA	January 1954	11 July 1960	41-33507 (USAAF), EX543/'BO', H.68 (RAF), 4KA shot down over Matadi-Tshimpi during Operation Mangrove.
H-203	88-13607	IIa/6C/4KA	November 1953	October 1960	41-33761 (USAAF), 4KA, crashed Bubanza (Urundi) August 1960. Used for spare parts by FAC.
H-204	88-12548	IIa/6C	November 1953	July 1956	41-33655 (USAAF) EX682/H.69 (RAF), withdrawn from use Kamina.
H-205	88-12321	IIa/6C	November 1953	January 1958	41-33628 (USAAF), EX655/H.96, withdrawn from use Kamina.
H-206	88-12322	IIa/6C/4K	November 1953	January 1958	41-33629 (USAAF), EX656/H.77, 4K prototype, withdrawn from use Kamina.
H-207	88-12765	IIa/6C/4KA	November 1953	August 1960	41-33672 (USAAF), EX699 (RAF), 4KA, belly landed Kaweka 25 July 1960 during Operation Mangrove.
H-208	88-12544	IIa/6C/4KA	November 1953	April 1962	41-33651 (USAAF), EX678/H.64 (RAF), 4KA. Crashed into Lake Nyanza, Usumbura, Ruanda, 23 April 1962.
H-209	88-10618	IIa/6C	November 1953	July 1956	41-33498 (USAAF), EX525/H.64 (RAF), withdrawn from use Kamina.
H-210	88-13399	IIa/6C/4KA	December 1953	July 1960	41-33726 (USAAF), EX753/ H.56 (RAF), 4KA, shot down near bridge over the River Inkisi, Thysville, 17 July 1960 during Operation Mangrove.
H-211	88-12337	IIa/6C	December 1953	July 1960	41-33644 (USAAF), EX671/H.55 (RAF), withdrawn from use Kamina.
H-212	88-1017	IIa/6C	November 1953	July 1960	41-33374 (USAAF), EX374/ '86' (RAF), withdrawn from use Kamina.
H-213	88-9641	IIa/6C/4KA	November 1953	May 1961	41-33218 (USAAF), EC245/ '81', (RAF), 4KA, crashed Usumbura, 10 March 1961.
H-214	88-10062	IIa/6C	December 1953	July 1956	41-33352 (USAAF), EX379/ '71' (RAF), withdrawn from use Kamina.
H-215	88-10250	IIa/6C	December 1953	July 1956	41-33393 (USAAF), EX420/H.57, (RAF), withdrawn from use Kamina.
H-216	88-10161	IIa/6C/4KA	December 1953	January 1961	41-33378 (USAAF), EX405/ 'B.U' (RAF), 4KA. Transferred to SAAF.
H-217	88-10621	IIa/6C	December 1953	July 1956	41-33501 (USAAF), EX528/ H.41 (RAF), withdrawn from use Kamina.
H-218	88-12764	IIa/6C	December 1953	July 1956	41-33671 (USAAF), EX698/ H.61, withdrawn from use Kamina.
H-219	88-9276	IIa/6C	January 1954	April 1954	41-33170 (USAAF), EX197 (RAF), crashed 3 September 1953. Used for spare parts.
H-220	88-13590	IIa/6C/4KA	November 1953	August 1962	1-33744 (USAAF), EX771/H.75 (RAF), test aircraft for 4KA version, transferred to FAC H-221 and 9T-P36.
H-221	88-13603	IIa/6C/4KA	December 1953	August 1962	41-33757(USAAF), EX784/H.62 (RAF), 4KA, transferred to FAC H-221 and 9T-PT37
H-222	88-12317	IIa/6C	November 1953	January 1958	41-33264 (USAAF), EX651/H.50, withdrawn from use at Kamina airbase.
H-223	88-10529	IIa/6C/4KA	December 1953	January 1961	41-3363 (USAAF), EX657/H.80 (RAF), served as part of the Nossin display team, 4KA, transferred to SAAF (7730).
H-224	88-10529	IIa/6C	December 1953	July 1956	41-33409 (USAAF), EX409/H.60, withdrawn from use Kamina.

Similarly to H-017, H-018 would be reintroduced into the Congo having been withdrawn in May 1958. Pictured here wearing its BAF colours, it would find its way back to the Congo through Cogea Nouvelle, a Belgian civil company operating out of Ostend. Pictured in flight over Brustem, Belgium, after the independence of the Congo H-18 became part of the FAK as KA-26. (Air Historical Team KLM/MRA courtesy of Belgianwings)

H-22, an armed 6D is pictured at Kamina on its way to Léopoldville. Formerly based in Burundi, it was among six Harvards (H-23, 34, 35, 220 and 221) sent to form the basis of the FAC in August 1962. Note that H-22 carries no nationality colours. (Marc Dahlhjelm via Leif Hellström courtesy of Belgianwings)

H-31 is pictured here at Ostend in 1959. Another aircraft handled by Cogeo Nouvelle after service with the BAF in the Belgian Congo, it would finish its career as KA-30 of the FAK. (Daniel Brackx)

H-31 pictured here as KA-30 of the FAK. Note the markings "KA:30.". (Albert Grandolini)

Two pilots (Frank Swietek left) of the FAF units stand in front of H-35 at Kigali, Rwanda in the early part of 1960. An armed Harvard, H-35 later became 9T-P35 of the FAC. (Frank Swietek courtesy of Belgianwings)

H-35's armaments can be seen in this photo. (Albert Grandolini)

H-35 is pictured here wearing the colours of the FAC and its new registration 9T-P35. To its left is the former H-37 now registered as 9T-P47. (Albert Grandolini)

H-37 at Brustem in the late 1950s. Yet another Harvard IIa ferried back to the Congo via Cogea Nouvelle, H-37 was integrated into the FAC as 9T-P47. Pictured above. (Hubert Sermon Collection courtesy of Belgianwings)

H-52 is pictured here at Brustem. A Harvard III, Cogea Nouvelle brought about H-52 serving with the FAK as KA-32. (Guy Destrebecq Collection courtesy of Belgianwings)

H-52 in its FAK livery of dark brown post-July 1960. Former RAF pilot Jimmy Hedges stands in front of the aircraft. (Daniel Brackx)

H-25, H-142, H-144 and H-221 fly in formation over the Belgian Congo. (Albert Grandolini)

PIPER L-18C SUPER CUB

A single-engine, two-seat monoplane produced by Piper Aircraft from 1949. Acquired by Belgium through the Mutual Defense Assistance Program (MDAP), on 2 June 1960 the Avi/FP received four examples that had previously served with the *Aviation Légère de l'Armée de Terre* (ALAT) *belge*.

Table 30: Piper L-18C Super Cub				
Registration	c/n	Date in	Date out	Service history
OL-L148	18-3222	August 1958	January 1960	53-4822 (USAF) 1954, then to Ndjili (January 1960), to FP as P-61 (April 1960).[37]
OL-L149	18-3223	August 1958	January 1960	53-4823 (USAF) 1954, then to Ndjili (January 1960), to FP (April 1960) and as P-62 to FP. Last civil registration G-BKTA (UK).[38]
OL-L152	18-3226	August 1958	February 1960	53-4826 (USAF) 1954, then to Ndjili (January 1960) and as P-63 to FP (April 1960).
OL-L153	18-3227	August 1958	June 1960	53-4827 (USAF), then to Ndjili in crates. Last civil registration G-BSGC (UK).[39]

Originally registered as OL-L148, this Piper Super Cub would go on to serve in the Congo and Ruanda (Rwanda) as P-61. (Daniel Brackx)

POTEZ-AIR FOUGA CM.170-1 MAGISTER

On 28 September 1958, the decision was taken to replace the BAF's fleet of T-6 Harvards with 45 French-made Fouga CM.170 Magisters for use at the EPA. First developed by Fouga in Béziers, France from 1948, in 1952 the Magister was fitted with two Turbomeca Marboré turbojet engines. Operating primarily as a trainer aircraft, the Magister provided close air support in the Six-Day War, the Western Sahara War and as part of the FAK. Allegedly used to bring down an aircraft carrying UN Secretary Dag Hammarskjöld in September 1961, a Magister was used against Irish peacekeeping forces at the Siege of Jadotville. As for the Belgian Congo, 20 of the 45 jets were withdrawn from Kamina when the Congo Crisis started in July 1960 (MT-1 to MT-18, MT-23 and MT-24), while during the same period six (MT-4, 6, 10, 14, 17 and 18) operating out of Ndjili were briefly used against armed rioters. In the later years of their service, MT-4, 6, 17 and 18 formed part of Belgium's aerobatic display team, the 'Red Devils'.

Table 31: Potez-Air Fouga CM.170-1 Magister				
Registration	c/n	Date In	Date Out	Service Record
MT-4	261	February 1960	June 2006	BAKA, Ndjili, then stored for Royal Army Museum at Landen, Belgium.
MT-6	263	March 1960	September 1977	BAKA, Ndjili, 'Red Devils', crashed Brustem 1976.
MT-10	267	March 1960	May 1965	BAKA, Ndjili, crashed Kerkom, Belgium, May 1965.
MT-14	271	April 1960	Feb 2003	BAKA, Ndjili, stored Beavechain, Belgium.
MT-17	274	May 1960	September 1969	BAKA, Ndjili 'Red Devils', written off Brustem, 1969.
MT-18	275	June 1960	October 1978	BAKA, Ndjili, 'Red Devils', stored Tel Aviv.

Fouga Magister MT-10
pictured at BAKA in June 1960.
(Frank Swietek courtesy of
Belgianwings)

SIKORSKY H-19 CHICKASAW (S-55)

A multi-purpose helicopter first produced in 1950. Made by US aircraft manufacturer Sikorsky, it was used by several air forces around the world and saw service in 1950s conflicts such as the First Indochinese War, the Korean War, the Malayan Emergency, and the Algerian War. Initially used for casevac, the French adapted the H-19 into a helicopter gunship in Algeria. As for the Belgian Congo, in 1959 the Belgian government purchased two H-19 helicopters through the MDAP that were to be used by the *Force Publique* in the Belgian Congo. One suffered damage and was left at Kitona on the Congo's independence (30 June 1960), while the other would be used by the FAK. Two more Sikorskys were transferred from SABENA in April 1960: one crashed after only a few days whereas the other became the property of the Congolese administration in July 1960.

Table 32: Sikorsky H-19 Chickasaw (S-55)				
Registration	c/n	Date in	Date out	Service history
S-41	55-1272	September 1959	July 1960	Abandoned at Kitona, its parts were used by UNOC forces. Still present Kitona 1963.
S-42	55-1276	September 1959	June 1960	Passed to FAK becoming KAT-42 in September 1960, it was captured, vandalised, and impounded by UNOC forces at Elisabethville, 28 August 1961. Transferred to UNOC but never reused.

Table 33: S-55				
Registration	c/n	Date in	Date out	Service history
S-43	55-839	01/03/1960	April 1960	OO-CWF (SABENA) 1955, used by Avi / FP (S-43) flew Sabena's colours.
S-44	55-840	01/03/1960	August 1960	OO-CWG (SABENA) 1955, used by Avi / FP (S-44), then FAC WH-01, WT-01.

S-41 was an H-19 Chickasaw that suffered damage at Kitona. Abandoned by the *Force Publique* on 4 April 1960, it was then used for spare parts by UNOC forces. (Hubert Sermon Collection courtesy of Belgianwings)

S-44 became WH-01 of the *Force Publique*. Subsequently it became WT-01 of the FAC. (Laurent Heyliger Collection courtesy of Belgianwings)

STAMPE-VERTONGEN SV-4B

A two-seat trainer biplane made from wood and with a canvas covering, at the beginning of the Second World War the Belgian military aviation possessed 24 examples (c/n 2201 to 2224) delivered before the invasion of Belgium on 10 May 1940. Transported to Oran-La Sénia in Algeria for storage, on 7 September 1940, 23 of the original 24 (one destroyed during the invasion by Nazi Germany) were handed over to French Vichy authorities. Then transported to Noisy-les-Bains, Algeria (now Ain Nouissy), the aircraft remained in the hands of Vichy forces until November 1942 and the invasion of Algeria by Allied forces. After testing, only seven of the 23 were sold to the Belgian Congo for 3.5 million French francs in February 1943 by the Belgian government in exile in London. After further transportation from Algeria to Casablanca, Morocco in August 1943, the aircraft were put in crates and were supposed to be sent to the Belgian Congo via Dakar, Senegal in October. Still in Dakar in July 1944, they finally arrived in the Belgian Congo a short time after for use by the FP. They were assigned the serials V41 to V47, or V40 to V46.[40]

Table 34: Stampe-Vertongen SV-4B				
Registration	c/n	Date in	Date out	Service record
V-41	-	1940	Unknown	Unknown
V-42	-	1940	Unknown	Unknown
V-43	-	1940	1948	Crashed into sand bank.
V-44	-	1940	1954	OO-CCN of the Léopoldville Flying Club, crashed 260/05/1955.
V-45	-	1940	Unknown	Unknown
V-46	-	1940	Unknown	Unknown
V-47	-	1940	Unknown	Unknown

SUD AVIATION SUD EST SE3130 ALOUETTE II

Produced by the *Société nationale de constructions aéronautiques Sud Aviation* (SNCASE), the Alouette II was a light helicopter first produced in 1957. The world's first helicopter powered by gas turbine, the Alouette II was used by several colonial forces and saw service in Algeria, Angola, Rhodesia, and South Africa.

Table 35: Sud Aviation Sud Est SE3130 Alouette II				
Registration	c/n	Date in	Date out	Service history
A-51[41]	1341/156C	April 1960	18/07/1960	Forced landing near Thysville and captured by ANC forces 18/07/1960. Pilots Ryckmans and Kervyn killed. Recovered by UNOC and transferred to FAC (WL-04).[42]
A-52	1365/166C	April 1960	18/07/1960	A-52, then KAT-52. Captured and vandalised by UNOC forces at Elisabethville, 28 August 1961.
A-53	1366/167C	April 1960	18/07/1960	A-53, then KAT-53. Captured and vandalised by UNOC forces at Elisabethville, 28 August 1961. Possibly used by FAC.

A-52 of the BAF subsequently became part of the FAK as KAT-52. It is pictured here carrying Major Guy Weber (front), and Jean-Marie Crèvecoeur. Weber had been appointed as military advisor to Katangan president Moïse Tshombe while Crèvecoeur was the commander of the Katangese Gendarmes. (Albert Grandolini)

7

Trouble Brews in the Belgian Congo

During and after the Second World War, the FP assured its role of safeguarding the Belgian Congo's territorial integrity and maintaining public order within the colony's boundaries. Over the past five years there had been instances whereby lethal force had to be used against striking miners at Jadotville (Likasi), Elisabethville and Kipushi in December 1941 and, as a sign of things to come, the FP was obliged to intervene against mutinous FP soldiers in Luluabourg (Kananga) in February 1944. In the first instance security forces killed over a hundred miners, and in the second over a hundred FP mutineers were dispatched in brutal fashion by their former comrades in arms. A last example of when the FP exacted its duties to the letter occurred at Matadi in November 1945 when armed repression of a strike by dock workers led to seven of them losing their lives.[1]

Despite isolated incidents such as those mentioned above, since the demise of Léopold II's regime the Belgian Congo had made significant progress regarding the health, education, and safety of the colony's inhabitants. This progress made mainly in the 1920s and 1930s and leading to the emergence of a Congolese elite classified by colonial authorities as *évolués*, if there certainly was room for improvement in the lives of rural workers in particular, living standards for Congolese residing and working in urban areas outstripped those of the indigenous populations of British colonies. Annual income per capita in the Belgian Congo was estimated at £27 in 1955,[2] and by comparison, it was £22 in Nigeria, £21 in Kenya, and £20 in Uganda.[3] As well as colonial authorities having provided primary schools in far higher number than in British West Africa, British East Africa, and French colonies in sub-Saharan Africa by the early 1950s,[4] this decade saw the initiation of a Ten-Year Plan

The *Force Publique* of the 1950s had become a disciplined military unit whose main role was to uphold the authority of the Belgian Congolese government. (Albert Grandolini)

Ford's M8 Greyhound was the only armoured vehicle used by the FP in the 1950s. (Open source)

racial lines. In fact, if there was segregation, it appears that this was a matter of convention: inter-racial marriage and social intercourse were not prohibited; and there were no laws excluding the Congolese from employment in certain sectors to perform certain roles.[8] This was true especially for *évolués*; many of whom were employed as white-collar workers in industry or banking, and owned businesses. Indeed, Joseph Tshombe, the father of Katangan leader and prime minister of the Democratic Republic of the Congo (DRC) was said to be the Congo's first millionaire having made his fortune from importing manioc from Kasaï into Katanga.[9] Other Congolese worked as civil servants. This was the case for future president Joseph Kasa-Vubu who was employed as a clerk in the Finance Department of the Governor General's Office.

In spite of progress having been made as far as welfare and employment opportunities for the Congolese, it is significant that the indigenous population was deprived of political representation until 1957. It being also significant that the Congolese were denied access to a university education in the Congo until 1954 and the creation of the Louvanium University, perhaps the most

that saw £45 million spent on roads, around £104 million spent on river, lake, rail, and air communications, more than £21 million on providing power, £16 million on improving water supplies, and £54 million on improving housing for civil servants, some of whom were Congolese.[5] The results of this investment already becoming clear by 1958 the indigenous share of the national income increased from 46 percent in 1950 to 58 percent.[6] As incomes increased, so did the desire to enjoy a Western lifestyle: the Congolese began to purchase electrical goods, textiles, alcohol, and even cars. On top of these developments in terms of salaries, the Congolese also benefitted from family allowances, illness and accident insurance and pensions. As far as the latter is concerned, a decree issued on 6 June 1956 made the Belgian Congo the first colonial power to institute pensions for native employees in private enterprises in sub-Saharan Africa.[7] Another area where vast improvements were made in the 1950s in the Congo is that of race relations. Whereas South Africa and some southern US states still enforced by law what is known informally as the "colour bar", in the Belgian Congo there was no official government policy implementing separation along

important factor linked to the political agitation that arose in 1946 was the fact that most Congolese employed in white-collar sectors were employed by dint of the fact that they could provide something for the colonial authorities. Only a relatively small number of Congolese owning businesses, there were no Congolese doctors, dentists, or professional lawyers. In short, in the years leading up to the introduction of political representation the Congolese were not to take full advantage of reforms. This aspect of life in the Congo not overlooked by Congolese cultural or educative associations such as the *Association des Anciens Elèves des Pères de Scheut* (ADAPES), or several other old-boy networks,[10] this base provided the platform for the appearance of movements committed to obtaining what they perceived as a fairer society would emerge. In this respect, workers associations such as the *Association du Personnel Indigène du Congo Belge et du Ruanda-Urundi* (APIC) or the *Union des Intérêts Sociaux Congolais* (UNISCO) were created,[11] and from a political point of view one of the most prominent associations was the *Alliance des Bakongo* (ABAKO). Created by Edmond Nzaza-Landu and starting life in 1950 as a cultural association promoting the history and

Baudouin of Belgium visits the Congo in 1955. His accession to the throne in 1951 corresponded to a time when colonial authorities were implementing a plan to improve the living standards of the Belgian Congo's indigenous populations. (Author's collection)

Joseph Kasa-Vubu became chairman of the ABAKO in 1955. A figurehead in the early days of Congolese politics, he became the country's first president, a role he held from June 1960 to November 1965. (Belgian National Archives)

Continuing with this strategy of setting up localised political connections over the next three years, the ABAKO was thrown into the arena of national politics in 1956 after a report by Belgian academic Anton Arnold Van Bilsen suggested that the Congo could achieve independence following a 30-year transitional period.[14] Conciliatory in tone and content, Van Bilsen criticised Belgium's "half-century domination" of the Congo, its "outmoded methods", and its failure to train doctors, veterinarians, and engineers. In his view, the period of political emancipation of the Congo [was] opening and that Congolese independence was "inevitable".[15] Though a group of Catholic Africans including Joseph Ileo mirrored Van Bilsen's comments in a manifesto published in July 1956 in *Conscience Africaine*, their comments were vague in nature insofar as the role Belgian political parties would play in the emancipation programme.[16] The manifesto stated political institutions in the Belgian Congo would undergo progressive change, and a nominative system would be replaced by one which saw the Congolese elect their own representatives. Moreover, Congolese advisory bodies which currently performed a purely consultative role would receive more authority in decision-making so that they would be ready to form a government when the time came. It also argued against the creation of political parties in the Congo seeing them as "a useless evil" due to their different political objectives. What was needed at this time, according to Ileo, was union and not division.[17] Although this manifesto was the first demonstration of the Congolese desire to determine their own future, Ileo's thoughts were highly criticised in a "Counter-Manifesto" published by ABAKO in August 1956. As evidence of division within the ABAKO camp and differences between Ileo and Kasa-Vubu, it rejected out of hand the idea that Belgium should help shape the Congo. Stating that Van Bilsen's plan should be "annihilated" as it would only retard Congolese independence further, this manifesto saw the differing objectives of political parties as "dangerous but necessary in a democracy".[18] Instead, and reflecting its own ideology, it put forward the suggestion that groups which were linked historically, ethnically, and linguistically should be part of a Congolese Federation.[19]

By the time political future of the Congo had started to swing in favour of the Congolese, events taking place in the international arena were to have a substantial influence on the evolution of the question of independence. While pressure was put on colonising nations to promote the concepts of equal rights and self-determination for non-self-governing territories, perhaps the most significant boost to national and political awareness in the Congo was the rise in popularity of Pan-Africanism. Since its creation in 1900, the influence of a movement founded by Trinidadian lawyer Henry Sylvester Williams reached the shores of the African

traditions of Kikongo-speaking Congolese, by 1955 it had become the most influential driving force behind obtaining independence for the Congo.[12] Chaired by Joseph Kasa-Vubu, it had received official recognition from the Belgian authorities soon after its creation and from there the ABAKO sought to spread an influence which had to that point been limited to geographical areas where there were the highest concentrations of Bakongo tribesmen. Between 1951 and 1953, the ABAKO extended its areas of activity from Léopoldville to Matadi and Thysville. This was done to establish links with co-operatives, youth groups and student associations.[13]

continent via Kwame Nkrumah. After studying in the United States and Britain where he had honed his political philosophy, in 1945 Nkrumah co-hosted the Fifth Pan-African Congress, which was held in Manchester from 15–21 October. Attended by 90 delegates, with 26 from Africa, the objective of the congress was to discuss the issues facing a large part of the African continent in respect of the remits of the UN charter. After one week of talks, it was resolved that imperialism and the monopolisation of "private wealth and industry for profit alone" should be condemned, and that every option was open when it came to the question of achieving political and economic independence.[20]

Looking on as Ghana became the first sub-Saharan African nation to reach these goals was Patrice Emery Lumumba. Born into humble surroundings Onalua in the Kasaï province in 1925, Lumumba belonged to the Batetela ethnic group, known for its resistance to Belgian colonial authority. Although, Lumumba was not a gifted child from an intellectual point of view, his assertive temperament, and his refusal to accept the authority of the teachers saw him expelled from Methodist and Catholic missionary schools. In 1944 Lumumba moved to Stanleyville in the Congo's Eastern Province where he obtained work as a postal clerk in the civil service. Shortly after, Lumumba began to take an interest in Congolese affairs and in 1952 he joined the *Association des évolués de Stanleyville* and the *Batetela de Léopoldville*. In each case, he furthered his political ambitions by transforming these socio-cultural associations into political groups by opposing the majority of the often-docile members.[21] Committed to improving race relations and a supporter of the creation of the Belgo-Congolese community expounded by *Conscience Africaine*, in 1956 Lumumba was invited to Brussels to meet King Baudouin. Considered as a potential ministerial advisor, Lumumba's political career came to a brief halt that same year when he was imprisoned for allegedly having misappropriated public funds. By the time Lumumba was released some 14 months later, his political ideology had changed from being supportive of a transitional period to wanting independence for the Congo as soon as possible. Identifying his own struggles with authority with the struggles faced by the Congolese as a nation,[22] on 5 October 1958 Lumumba joined the burgeoning *Mouvement National Congolais* (MNC).

Lumumba's rapid emergence as a force in nationalist politics was recognised almost immediately by some of Africa's most radical leaders when – to replace Kasa-Vubu as the Congolese delegate – he was invited to attend the First All-African People's Conference held in Accra, Ghana in December 1958. The conference brought together 300 delegates representing 65 organisations from 28 African countries, and strong representation came from North African countries which had obtained, or were in the process of obtaining, independence. West, East and Central African countries all had significant delegations as was the United States.[23] Its delegates included Eslanda Robeson and Shirley Graham Du Bois, the wife of W.E.B. Du Bois, the Pan-Africanist founder of the National Association for the Advancement of Coloured People (NAACP) in 1909.

When the time came for Lumumba to address the delegates, he demonstrated exactly why he was held in such high esteem. Considering the founding of the MNC as "a decisive step for the Congolese people as they move toward emancipation" in respect of the Universal Declaration of the Rights of Man and UN Charter, the MNC wished to "create a modern democratic state" which would grant its citizens "freedom, justice, social peace, tolerance, well-being and equality with no discrimination whatsoever".[24] Verbally

Patrice Lumumba was an adept of Pan-Africanist policies. An ideology that saw African cultural heritage as distinct from Western culture, it rejected colonialism and called for the reestablishment of African societies in Africa.

Moïse Tshombe was the son of a wealthy businessman and the chairman of the CONAKAT. With financial and political links to European businesses and business owners in Katanga, Tshombe opposed Pan-Africanism and advocated a continuation of relations with Belgium. (Albert Grandolini)

attacking the "injustices" and the "stupid superiority complex"[25] of the colonists, Lumumba's message must have been music to the ears of other Pan-Africanists such as Nkrumah, Kenneth Kaunda and Hastings Banda. Despite ethnic differences and the boundaries that separated [African nations], all had the "same awareness", the same "anguished soul", and the same "anxious desire" to free the African continent of fear and of colonist domination.[26] Foreshadowing the problems which lay ahead, however, Lumumba also warned that the factitious nature of a Congolese nation divided along tribal and religious lines was a serious hindrance to what he described

Widespread rioting started in Léopoldville on 4 January 1959. Taking place after a meeting organised by Joseph Kasa-Vubu was banned by authorities in the Belgian Congo, in this photo an officer and soldiers of the FP are seen confronting rioters. (Albert Grandolini)

All types of weapons were used by the rioters in a show of their anger at a lack of political representation. (Albert Grandolini)

as the "flowering of a harmonious and fraternal African society".[27] For a man with little academic training, Lumumba's own political awareness and his ability to analyse the divisive nature of Congolese society and politics were unerringly accurate: discordant opinions had been voiced in reaction to the manifestos issued by *Conscience Africaine* and the ABAKO, and two new political parties – the *Centre de Regroupement African* (CEREA) in North Kivu, and the *Conféderation des associations tribales du Katanga* (CONAKAT) – had just been created. Both were tribal and both represented the interests of regional populations.[28]

Taking advantage from the MNC being seen as the only political representative of the nation as a whole and taking on the role of a government-in-waiting, two weeks after the Accra Conference, Lumumba organised a meeting of MNC supporters in Léopoldville. Through a denunciation of Belgium's policy of divide and rule in the Congo, Lumumba now confirmed that he possessed the characteristics and the vision that were needed to lead that very same government. Also showing that he was ready to fulfil this role was Joseph Kasa-Vubu. His party having won a majority of seats in the municipal elections held in December 1957 – the first elections in which the Congolese were allowed to participate. In January 1959 Kasa-Vubu also convened a meeting of his supporters which was due to be held at the Young Men's Christian Association headquarters in Léopoldville. Warned by Belgian officials that if the meeting became

political Kasa-Vubu would be held responsible and gaining the impression that the meeting was banned, on 3 January Kasa-Vubu then attempted to postpone the meeting. Despite these attempts a large crowd of supporters from the Bakongo tribe gathered in front of the YMCA where further appeals from Kasa-Vubu failed to disperse them.[29] Rioting then broke out and the subsequent burning of cars and businesses, and attacks on whites and members of other tribes resulted in a death toll of somewhere between 49 and 500.[30] After the riots, Kasa-Vubu and two other ABAKO leaders were arrested and sent to Belgium for trial. This only exacerbated racial tensions in the Congo.[31] Later that year, in October, a meeting organised by Lumumba in Stanleyville (Kisangani) also left 70 people dead. The nature of the riots in Léopoldville and an atmosphere within which whites were becoming increasingly threatened with violence moved King Baudouin to make a speech on 13 January 1959 in which he recognised the rights of the Congolese to self-determination. On the same day, the Belgian government also announced that it would accompany the Congolese through a transitional period during which Congolese officials would be able to participate in executive and legislative procedures. Racial discrimination was to be abolished and there was to be an Africanisation of the administration.[32]

With political parties jostling for position in what was becoming a context characterised by inter-tribal dispute the Luluabourg Congress was organised in April 1959 where it was hoped that tribal electoral lists would be prohibited.[33] As rivalries continued throughout 1959, in December Baudouin made his first visit to the colony since 1955. While many observers admired the courage of the young monarch, others reacted with surprise and believed that the visit constituted a last throw of the dice in the effort to ease tensions between coloniser and colonised. A second congress between representatives of different Congolese parties was held in Bakuvu in eastern Congo between 6–8 January 1960 and the peaceful atmosphere of the meetings held between these dates set the stage for the talks between Belgian and Congolese that took place in Brussels between 20 January–20 February 1960. A second series of meetings took place from 26 April–16 May of the same year. It was in Brussels that the political and tribal rivalries that had led to so much division in the Congo from 1958 started to reappear. These divisions even included a split inside the MNC when, following disagreement between Lumumba and Albert Kalonji the latter created the *Mouvement National Congolais-Kalonji* (MNC-K). This had come about after Lumumba had lent support to the Lulua people in the Kasaï region of the Congo. A Baluba, Kalonji opposed any measure that would give an advantage to a bitter enemy such as the Lulua. Along with ABAKO and the *Parti Solidaire Africain* (PSA), or African Solidarity Party, Kalonji opposed Lumumba's concept of a unitary state governed from Léopoldville and, instead, argued that the Congo should be a loose federation of separate states.[34] Despite the differences in opinion, participants at the conference nevertheless agreed that independence should be set for the 30 June 1960 and that provincial and legislative elections should be held a month earlier.

In an endorsement of his popularity in the Orientale, Kivu and Kasaï provinces, Patrice Lumumba was to emerge triumphant in these elections. Obtaining 33 of a possible 137 seats available, and well ahead of Kasa-Vubu and Kalonji, Lumumba now found himself the most influential and powerful man in Congolese politics. While news of the returns in the elections brought joy to Lumumba's supporters, for Europeans in the Congo the results cemented pre-election fears that they would become the target of anti-colonial sentiment. Indeed, in Lumumba's stronghold of Stanleyville, some Europeans were insulted and stoned, leading them to describe the leader of the MNC as 'most dangerous'.[35] In other parts of the Congo, after similar scenes took place, many Europeans were reported to be sending their wives and children away from the Congo after lists of Europeans and their residences were published in African newspapers. Allegedly, this was even the case in Katanga, a province hostile to Lumumba.[36] Sharing the opinion that Lumumba in a position of power was dangerous and believing that Lumumba would seek to impose himself on Congolese Cabinet affairs, the Belgian officials sent to oversee the transition from colony to independence were nevertheless wary of attempting to exclude Lumumba from any government formed through the provisions of the recently drawn up constitution.[37]

This type of political manoeuvring continued throughout June 1960 with, on the one hand, Lumumba attempting to form a government and, on the other, Joseph Kasa-Vubu talking of establishing a separate Mukongo province. Moïse Tshombe of Katanga also threatened to secede immediately if an amendment giving the province greater representation in the Congolese parliament was not added to the draft constitution.[38] In turn, in north-eastern Katanga, Jason Sendwe of the *Association Générale des Baluba de Katanga* (BALUBAKAT) was also declaring its determination to set up a separate state, one that would act in opposition to Tshombe's CONAKAT.[39] Here, the political situation worsened when tribal conflict between the Lulua and Baluba tribes led to a state of emergency being declared on 14 June. Further political wrangling continued over the next few days as political rivals jockeyed

Before independence was declared officially, Patrice Lumumba met FP commander General Emile Janssens to discuss the future of the Congo's armed forces. (Albert Grandolini)

for position in the Congo's upper and lower houses. This included Lumumba opponent Joseph Ileo being elected head of the Congolese Senate over the Lumumba-supported Alexandre Mahamba. Despite opposition to his own candidates, in a sign of magnanimity Lumumba continued in his efforts to form a broadly based Cabinet that included rivals. Lumumba, whose party had gained control over the House of Representatives, was then invited by Walter Van der Meersh to form a government. Political compromise was reached through the composition of Lumumba's first Cabinet. On 23 June, with Lumumba holding the dual role of Prime Minister and Defence Minister, concessions were made to CONAKAT by putting this party in charge of the Ministry of Economics. As for other appointments, Lumumbists Justin Bomboko became Foreign Minister and Thomas Kanza was named as the Congo's United Nations delegate. The composition of the Congo's first government was completed with the election of Joseph Kasa-Vubu as Head of State on 24 June and to all appearances the country could now look forward to officially gaining its independence less than a week later.

One of the most iconic images connected to the independence of the Congo on 30 June 1960. Here, a spectator seizes Baudouin's ceremonial sword symbolising the transfer of power from coloniser to colonised. (Albert Grandolini)

Below this surface of optimism though lay simmering tensions that were soon to throw the Congo into chaos.

Refusing to accept that the Congo had fallen into the hands of extremists wishing to impose a unitary structure over the country and having seen BALUBAKAT political rival Jason Sendwe appointed State Commissioner for the province, Moïse Tshombe flew back to Elisabethville on 23 June. The same day, Tshombe declared that he was withdrawing his support for Lumumba.[40] With fears that Katanga would secede, on 28 June, Lumumba had met with FP chief

Lieutenant General Janssens and, in the scope of article 250 of an agreement put in place between Congo and Belgian governments,[41] it was decided that Katanga would be brought into the union through force if necessary.[42] Secondly, during an impromptu speech given by Lumumba in the *Palais de la Nation* on Independence Day itself, Lumumba launched into a violent denunciation of Belgian rule in front of representatives from Asian and African countries as well as the world's press. For some, this was when "trouble started", and the Crisis began.[43]

8

Belgium's Military Response to Civil Disorder in the Congo, 1959–1960

The demonstrations that began on 4 January 1959 in Léopoldville were in many ways a signal to colonial authorities in the Belgian Congo that political change in the colony was on its way. Taking place after a rally by supporters of Joseph Kasa-Vubu had been broken up by the FP, they were a precursor to much more serious violence that took place in July 1960 and which brought an end to the *Force Publique* as the Belgian Congo's peacekeepers. Paradoxically, it would be members of the FP themselves that would instigate the rioting in this instance.

As the rioters burned and looted their way through the capital from 4 January 1959, plans were already afoot to bring back public order. General Janssens had called upon the 2nd Group FP to uphold its role and to cease the disorder, and soon Henrik Cornelis, the Governor General and the commander of Cométro called in the

3rd Battalion of paracommandos based at BAKA. An advance party of paratroopers arrived at Ndjili aboard a C-47 on 5 January, and its role was to secure Léopoldville's administrative centre as well as the aerodrome at N'Dolo. This the first time metropolitan troops had been used to quell civil disorder in the colony, the 2nd Battalion of paracommandos arrived later that day.[1] The following day, Cométro gave the order for six unarmed T-6s and two Bristol Sycamores rushed from BAKA to N'Dolo. A Sikorsky S-55 loaned by SABENA also joined operations as DH Doves of the FP.[2] The mission of this combined force was to act as observation aircraft and to survey areas where the potential for further disorder was at its highest. These areas included the areas of Léopoldville populated by Kasa-Vubu's Bakongo supporters, but also in the Madimba Territory to the south of the capital and in Thysville, a city situated some 95 miles west of

Two of the BAF's Bristol Sycamores were used as reconnaissance aircraft during the riots that took place in Léopoldville in early January 1959. Here, B-1 is pictured at BAKA attended by Congolese ground crew. Two hundred and fifty Congolese technicians were trained at Kamina from 1949 to 1960. (Daniel Brackx)

The H-19 Chickasaw coded S-42 was acquired by the Avi / FP in September 1959. In August 1960, it became KAT-42 of the FAK. (Frank Swietek courtesy of Belgianwings)

This Piper Super Cub was one of three acquired by the Avi/FP in April 1959. Liveried all yellow and operating out of Ndjili, P-61, P-62, and P-63 were used for reconnaissance. (Albert Grandolini)

Nossin, and a parachute drop involving C-47s.[4] Despite the celebration of Belgian air power in Africa, the memory of the January riots were still fresh in the mind and soon the question of whether to arm aircraft in the case of lager scale popular insurrection came to the table. Initially, six Harvards used by the EPA were chosen to undergo testing at BAKA and were fitted with two 7.62mm machineguns, two Alcan 261 bomb racks and two Matra 13 rocket launchers by Congolese weapons technicians. Designated 4KAs (See list of Harvards, *Chapter 6*), what became the *Flight Appui Feu* (FAF), or Flight Assistance Fire, initially became a wing of the BAF's search and rescue team at BAKA.[5]

Léopoldville and home to Camp Hardy, one of the FP's largest bases in the Congo. If the FP was able to restore order in Léopoldville over the coming days, on 14 January further incidents took place in the port of Matadi where shops were looted. The troops of the FP put on high alert, more rioting occurred in the Cataractes District (between Matadi and Stanley Pool), but cooperation between spotter planes and ground forces quickly brought the situation under control. The need for the FP to have more light aircraft at its disposal becoming clear, in April 1959 FP HQ hired a Piper Club and a Piper PA-12 Super Cruiser from the Aéroclub de Léopoldville for use by the Avi / FP and acquired three Piper Super Cubs. Piloted by Avi / FP Commandants Deschepper, Delcourt, Diericx and Rahier, these aircraft were used for reconnaissance.[3] 1959 also saw the Avi / FP acquire two H-19 Chickasaws coded S-41 and S-42. Placed under the command of Commandant Kervyn de Meerendre, S-42 would be integrated into the FAK in August 1960.

After visiting the colony in April 1959 to take stock of its military situation, the Belgian Minister for Defence Arthur Gilson returned in July as part of celebrations marking the 10th anniversary of the establishment of the air force base at Kamina. The celebrations included a fly-past during which three Harvards denoted smoke bombs displaying the colours of the Belgian flag (black, yellow, and red), an aerial display provided by Harvards led by Major Georges

September and October of 1959 were two months during which dissatisfaction amongst the Congolese was on the increase. On 27 September two Congolese political parties – the *Parti Solidaire Africain* and the ABAKO – called for a boycott of local elections in protest against restrictions imposed by colonial authorities; 28 people were hospitalised after the FP broke up a religious meeting at Matadi on 12 October; and tribal clashes between members of the Lulua and Baluba tribes had broken out on 11–12 October in Kananga.[6] Confronted by a worsening situation, the next day the Belgian Committee of the Chiefs of Staff (COCEM) met in Brussels and held a series of discussions that lasted until 3 November. One of the first items on the agenda were the latest series of riots carried out by ABAKO supporters in the Belgian Congo, and updates on their activities were provided by the head the Belgian Congo's security forces, (*Sûreté Coloniale*), Colonel Frédéric Vandewalle. A FP officer known later for helping to organise the secession of Katanga and for planning a march from Katanga to Stanleyville to rescue hostages held by the Simba during the Congo Crisis, Vandewalle convened a meeting between Cométro and General Janssens in Brussels in an attempt to find a solution to the chaos currently taking place in the colony. Janssens denied that the FP had lost control of the situation

The CM.170 serial-numbered MT-1 was the first Fouga Magister delivered to BAKA. (Jacques Schelfaut courtesy of Belgianwings)

A member of the Bayaka tribe is pursued by children with sticks in a predominantly Bakongo district of Léopoldville. (author's collection)

for legislative elections to elect members for the future Congolese parliament. These due to be held in May 1960, far from having a calming effect on the Congo's social context, inter-ethnic tension mounted as each political party jostled to gain dominance. On the streets of Léopoldville this led to a violent exuberance whereby the supporters of one particular tribe handed out brutal beatings to those of another.

The plans for Congolese independence not having an imminent impact on the FP or the Belgian forces based in Kamina, on 22 January 1960 the first Fouga Magister

and affirmed that order would be restored as soon as possible. This included stationing a company of the FP's 4th Commando Battalion at Kitona air base and at Camp Stanley in Stanley Pool.[7] Chaos continued, however. The FP clashed with Congolese nationalists in Stanleyville between 29–31 October leaving up to 75 dead, and there was rioting in Léopoldville following a speech given by Patrice Lumumba on 30 October. The FP leaving 29 rioters dead,[8] the FP then had to deal with the beginnings of the Rwandan Revolution. A precursor to the Rwandan genocide of 1994, in 1959 Colonel Guillaume Logiest sent FP reinforcements to Usumbura and Kigali to quell Hutu rebels intent on killing Tutsis.

The Rwandan Revolution seeing the country transition from a Belgian colony with a Tutsi monarch to a Hutu-dominated autonomous republic in 1962, as for the question of independence for the Belgian Congo – and as seen in the previous chapter – the objective of the Brussels Round Table Conference that began on 3 January 1960 led to the adoption of 16 resolutions relating to the future of the country and fixed the date for it to gain autonomy as 30 June. The resolutions becoming known as the *Loi Fondamentale*, or Fundamental Law, one important factor was that Belgium was to retain control of its air and naval bases even after independence. Another aspect that came out of the meetings concerned the date

CM.170 arrived in the Congo where they were due to replace some of the older T-6 Harvards. The Fouga in question serial-numbered MT-1, its arrival at BAKA aboard a Fairchild C-119G Flying Boxcar corresponded to the creation of an Instruction and Transport Wing (WIT) comprising seven C-47s already stationed at BAKA and six other C-119s made available by the 15th Wing Air Transport of the BAF stationed at Melsbroek in Belgium. With 37 T-6s still based at BAKA, of which seven were 4KAs, the creation of Fire Assistance Flights was accelerated so that they could also join the WIT and take part in the FP's public order duties should the need arise.[9]

As yet, no Fouga or T-6 pilot had tested the aircrafts' armaments outside firing ranges. This said, regular testing was carried out and the weapons systems aboard the aircraft were maintained to be battle-ready. As for the pilots, an appeal was made for volunteers in Belgium who would be prepared to take part in the forming of the FAF. A first group arrived on 16 February 1960. Having been trained to fly jets, officers such as Ss-Lt. Frank Swietek of the BAF's 10th Wing and Ss.-Lt. Gilles of the 2nd Wing were provided with training to readjust themselves to flying propeller-driven aircraft such as the T-6. Receiving this training from instructors based at BAKA, the flights were made using H-210, H-213 and H-22.[10] Used in anger for the first time on 24 February 1960, the FAF's mission was to

Kamina (AP907) had a varied career. Starting life in 1938 as the Polish cargo ship *Lewant III*, it was captured by the Wehrmacht in 1940 and renamed the *Hermann von Wissman* after the German explorer who had once worked for Léopold II and who became an FP officer. Serving in Finland, Poland, and Norway from 1943, the ship then acted as a support vessel for German submarines during the Battle of the Bulge. Scuttled in Norway in 1945, the ship became *HMS Harold* before being bought by the Belgian navy in 1950. From here, it acted as a transport ship in the Korean War and carried Belgian personnel to Ostend in October 1960. (Belgian-navy.be)

M/F904 *De Brouwer* was an Algerine-class minesweeper built by Hartland and Wolff in Belfast. Commissioned in September 1942 as HMS *Spanker*, it swept mines around Gibraltar, Malta, along the Italian and French coasts as well as in the Adriatic. Renamed the BNS *De Brouwer* in 1953, it arrived in Banana on 10 June 1960 after a stop-off at Lobito, Angola. (Author's collection)

Also built by Harland and Wolff, the *Georges Lecointe* was commissioned as HMS *Cadmus* in 1942. An Algerine-class minesweeper, it supported the Allied landings in North Africa (Operation Torch) as well as serving in Greece. Acquired by the Belgian navy in 1950 and renamed *Georges Lecointe*, this vessel acted as the flagship for Belgian naval operations in the Congo. (Belgian-navy.be)

be sent to Kanaga in the Kasai Province, an area of the Congo in which a state of emergency had been declared in view of continuing strife between the Lulua and Baluba tribes. The role of the FAF being to patrol areas at risk of witnessing bloody encounters, they were accompanied by elements of the WIT carrying the 6th Battalion of the FP from Watsa. The FP's 12th Battalion also arriving in the region by train from Elisabethville, another development that took place in the early quarter of 1960 was the reinforcement of Cométro forces through the training of the FP's *2nd Bataillon Commando* (paracommando battalion) at Kitona and its *1st Batallion Parachutiste* that was to be based at BAKA. A second development was the implementation of a military dispositive intended to protect Europeans should they be attacked after the independence of the Congo. General Janssens not believing this was necessary, and finally only three battalions of the Belgain Army were sent to BAKA, on 16 May 1960 Belgian Prime Minister expressed his dismay at the deterioration of the situation in the Congo and appointed Walter Ganshof van der Meersh as Minister in charge of general affairs in Africa. A Belgian jurist and lawyer who had once competed as a member of a four-man bobsleigh team at the 1928 Winter Olympics held in St. Moritz, Switzerland, his role was to work alongside Arthur Gilson to examine in which ways soldiers from Belgium's 1st Regiment of Grenadiers (*1er régiment de grenadiers*) and from the 1st Company of the Chasseurs Ardennais (*1ère compagnie de marche des Chasseurs Ardennais*) could be used to the greatest effect. Based at BAKA and BAKI (Kitona),[11] both regiments saw action from July 1960

Constructed in Blyth, England, the *A.F. Dufour* (M903) was commissioned as HMS *Fancy* in November 1943. Preparing the southern coast of England in view of the invasion of Normandy, she served in the Adriatic and Venice before acquisition by the Belgian navy in 1952. Based in Banana from September 1957, *A.F. Dufour* acted as a training ship for Congolese forces. (Belgian-navy.be)

Starting life as HMS *Rosario* in July 1943 and constructed by Harland and Wolff, in 1944 the ship served off the coast of southern France in preparation for Operation Dragoon. Decommissioned by the Royal Navy in 1947, the ship was acquired by the Belgian Navy in January 1953. Sent to the Belgian Congo in 1958, *De Moor* (M905) was designated as a support vessel for scientific research carried out in the Congo Basin. (Belgian-navy.be)

a rather good-natured affair soured very quickly as the rank and file of the FP realised that hierarchically speaking their situation remained the same and that there would not be promotions across the board nor subsequent pay rises. Effectively, to assist the Congo's new government in the task of assuring its responsibilities, on 29 June the Treaty of Friendship, Assistance and Cooperation was signed by Belgian Prime Minister Gaston Eyskens, Belgian Foreign Minister Pierre Wigny, Lumumba, and Congolese Minister of Foreign Affairs Justin Bomboko. The treaty stipulated that Belgian civil servants in the Congo and FP officers would remain at their posts while continuing to be paid by the Belgian government.[12] Moreover, it stated that Belgian troops would continue to be stationed at BAKA and BAKI until such time that the administration of these bases could be handed over to the Congolese government. There were political factors, too. Many FP troops were dismayed that the unpopular Colonel van Hoorebeke had been appointed by Lumumba to serve as Janssens's second-in-command, and there was also dissatisfaction amongst troops in the Equateur and Kasai provinces who had hoped to see their respective political leaders (Jean Balikongo and Albert Kalonji) assigned to posts in Lumumba's Cabinet.[13]

To express their anger, on the morning of 4 July 1960 workers in Coquilhatville (now Mbandaka) laid down their tools in protest against Lumumba's appointments. The FP was sent to break up the strike and restore order, and in its last ever public order action it opened fire on protesters, killing nine.[14] While this was taking place, back at Camp Léopold II one NCO began spreading the rumour that as the Congo was now independent his fellow soldiers no longer had to take orders from Belgian officers. Rapidly demoted by Janssens who arrived at the camp at 17.00 hours, the NCO and two others were placed in detention.[15] The following day, Janssens underlined in black and white the fact that independence had changed little for the FP. Making his point clearer by chalking "Before Independence = After Independence" on a blackboard, discontent among the soldiers spread to Camp Hardy at Thysville where units of the FP's 4th Brigade mutinied against their white officers on 6 July. Some of them and their families severely beaten, Lumumba ordered the 2nd Infantry Battalion of the FP to intervene at Camp Léopold to stamp out the possibility of any further disruption. Stationed

as the Congo descended into chaos. Notwithstanding complaints from Patrice Lumumba who demanded the withdrawal of Belgian troops from the Congo after their arrival on 18 May, a final measure intended to increase the strength of the FP and Belgian forces already present in the Congo was taken by Gilson in June 1960 when he ordered a small naval task force to be assembled at the port of Banana. This force comprised the naval auxiliary ship *Kamina*, and four coastal escort ships, the *De Brouwer*, the *Georges Lecointe*, the *A.F. Dufour*, and the *De Moor*.

The End of the FP

The security measures put in place by Belgian and Belgian Congolese authorities from May 1960 were greatly aided by the transfer of aviation from Belgium and the modification of equipment already stationed in the colony. The utility of these measures was to become evident from 5 July 1960, just one week after the Belgian Congo had transitioned to independence and become Congo-Léopoldville. Independence had been obtained peaceably, there were no major incidents surrounding the independence ceremony itself, and King Baudouin had left the country for Belgium with the sound of the national anthems of Belgium and of the newly independent state played as he boarded his plane at Ndjili. However, what began as

Belgians forced to flee the Congo after the mutiny of the FP that started on 5 July, and which signalled the end of an institution that had lasted 115 years. These Europeans make their way from Katanga into Northern Rhodesia. (Author's collection)

in Maniema, but part of the 4th Brigade, these troops refused to fight against their own.[16] Mutiny broke out in other FP garrisons across the Congo. The troops broke out of their camps, ransacked European businesses, and Europeans began to leave their homes in Thysville to escape the violence. Lumumba identified by the mutineers as the cause of their woes, the next stop was the capital. Here, they attempted to force their way into the Congolese parliament. Despite Lumumba then attempting to negotiate, with mutineers also surrounding his official residence in Léopoldville Lumumba found himself obliged to backtrack on the terms of the Treaty of Friendship on 8 July. Janssens, van Hoorebeke and all the FP's white officers were dismissed with Lumumba embarking on an Africanisation of the Congo's armed forces. Replacing Janssens with his ageing uncle, Victor Lundula, as commander-in-chief of the newly created *Armée Nationale Congolais* (ANC), or Congolese National Army, former FP *Sergent Major* Joseph-Désiré Mobutu was appointed its Chief of Staff.[17] The changes did little to calm the anger of the now ANC mutineers. Spreading east, the mutiny reached Kongolo in northern Katanga and Camp Massart in Elisabethville. The riots which included the gang-raping of women and children as young as 12 forced thousands of Europeans to seek refuge.[18] Many left the Congo by road or rail, fled to neighbouring Angola, or crossed the River Congo into Brazzaville. In Northern Rhodesia, there was talk of forming units of commandos to rescue Europeans fleeing Elisabethville. Congolese civilians in nearby Kabalo were also complicit in the mutiny: some attempted to stop the departure of a train to Elisabethville carrying 250 Europeans to safety and they joined riots which took place in the mining towns of Shinkolobwe and Kolwezi.[19] Another caught up in the chaos was CIA Chief of

Station, Larry Devlin. Arriving in Léopoldville on 10 July, he was mistaken for a Belgian and taken prisoner. Made to kiss the boots of his captors, unless he complied Devlin was told he would be shot.[20] The mayhem continuing, an estimated 26,000 Europeans left the Congo during the first days of the mutiny.[21]

Operation Mangrove

As several companies of infantry and a battalion of paracommandos made their way from Melsbroek to BAKA aboard aircraft of the BAF's 15th Transport Wing from 9 July, their mission given as the protection of Europeans in Elisabethville and Luluabourg,[22] the situation around the Congolese port of Matadi had gradually worsened, leaving hundreds of Europeans either stranded in the city or on vessels attempting to take them across the Congo River into Congo-Brazzaville. Not only had ill-timed industrial action by dock workers blocked their efforts to reach safety, to make matters far more perilous, they were under threat of attack by mutineers now controlling Camp Redjaf and other positions (Fuka-Fuka, and Kala Kala) that guarded the entrance to Matadi. Armed with eight 40mm Bofors canons, sixteen 20mm Oerlikon canons, and automatic weapons they were well equipped to resist attempts to dislodge them. To address this danger, on the morning of 10 July 1960 the commander of Cométro forces, Roger Gheysen, ordered that a naval task force be constituted. The main objective being to liberate the port so that infantry could be landed, Operation Mangrove also targeted the occupation of the port of Boma some 27 miles (45kms) upriver from Matadi. The Belgian ship *Petitjean* was to be used as a command centre, and four FAF Harvard T-6/4KAs based at Kitona were to be used alongside troops of the Ardennes Chasseur Regiment and a company of Prince Léopold's 12th Line Regiment. At Boma, the responsibility of quelling the mutiny fell to a company of the 6th Commando Battalion.

Operation Mangrove began at 0215 on 11 July 1960 when the Naval Task Group received orders from Cométro HQ. The *Petitjean* transporting its cargo of troops upriver in the direction of Matadi, four T-6s of the FAF took off from BAKI (Kitona) under orders to fly over positions held by the mutineers but not to attack. While three of the aircraft continued their journey up through the hills that surrounded the port, at 0900 one broke formation to observe the progress of the 6th Commando Battalion at Boma. The city having quickly been secured by forces commanded by Major Lemasson, in the meantime three Algerines accompanied by three vedettes also made their way upriver. At 1015 *Dufour* and the vedette *Ourthe* broke off and headed for the small port of Ango-Ango located on the east bank of the River Congo and approximately one and a half miles (2.5kms) downstream from Matadi. Unloading 58 soldiers of the 12th Line Regiment, their mission under the command of Lt. Vrolix was to cut off the road leading to Matadi and to disarm 144 Congolese mutineers based at a camp around half a mile away from Ang-Ango. This done, they were then to seize control of four AA Bofors held by the rebels. With the Algerine *Lecointe* and the vedettes *Rupel* and *Dender* reaching Matadi some 20 minutes later at 1045, the role of the Ardennes Chasseurs they were carrying was to attack Camp Redjaf, which 357 mutineers were preparing to defend. The assault force not benefitting from tactical surprise, heavy fighting ensued with exchanges made between the mutineers' artillery pieces and the guns of the *De Moor*.

Though used as a show of strength in early exchanges, the T-6s of the FAF provided fire assistance throughout Operation Mangrove. H-202 crashed after being hit and losing fuel some distance from the airfield at Matadi, and with two other aircraft suffering

Troops of the Ardennes Chasseurs on their way to quell the ANC mutiny in the Lower Congo during Operation Mangrove. (Author's collection)

Ardennes Chasseurs disembark on the quay at Ango-Ango. (Author's collection)

of the Congo. These attacks stopped only after Mobutu made a personal appeal for the violence to cease and after the intervention of both Kasa-Vubu and Lumumba.

Towards the End of (Official) Belgian Military Presence in the Congo

While Belgian troops were disembarking at Ango-Ango and Matadi, the two most important government officials in the newly independent Congo had, in effect, been seeking to resolve issues that were beginning to have an adverse effect on the future of the nation they now led. Both Katanga and the Kasai being Congolese provinces in which political discord with Lumumba's objectives of implementing centralised control was at its highest, and two provinces witnessing sustained violence, on 11 July the Congolese President and Prime Minister boarded a DH Heron and headed for Katanga via Luluabourg. After spending the night at the Luluabourg garrison, the two men awoke to discover that Moïse Tshombe had declared Katanga to be independent. Made furious by this decision, on 12 July he ordered the aircraft's pilot to take him to Elisabethville for a showdown with Tshombe. The DH Heron made a stopover at BAKA to refuel at 1700, but after learning that the Heron was not equipped for night flights, the two senior Congolese officials boarded a C-47 and around 2130

damage it soon became apparent that the aircraft was susceptible to enemy fire due to an absence of shielding. Their efficiency also reduced by a lack of air-to-ground communications equipment; despite their intentions they were unable to provide the necessary assistance to ground troops. Indeed, by this time the mutineers were receiving their own assistance in the shape of the ANC's 4th Brigade based at Thysville. Though a T-6 was used to attack one of its M-8 Greyhounds with rocket fire killing two, a further aspect that eventually led to Operation Mangrove failing in its objectives was the increase in attacks perpetrated by the ANC on Belgian citizens in the Lower Congo as retribution. The Belgian troops taking part in Operation Mangrove ordered back to ship, and having reembarked by nightfall, more attacks were made on Belgians in northern areas

their aircraft was ready to make its approach for landing at Luano airport (now Lubumbashi airport). A standoff then occurred with Katangan Minister of the Interior Godefroid Munongo refusing to give Lumumba permission to land and ordering that the airport's landing lights be switched off.[23]

The arrival of Belgian paratroopers at Ndjili Airport to assist in the evacuation of Belgian nationals on 13 July only aggravating Lumumba's temper even further, although his reaction to an increasingly complicated context can be explained to some extent by inexperience, it was to lead to a series of errors of judgement that would eventually see Lumumba's downfall. His first mistake was to break diplomatic relations with Belgium, the only country capable of providing the prime minister with the political leverage needed

H-210 is armed at Kitona Air Base (BAKI) during Operation Mangrove. (author's collection)

While Ardennes Chasseurs were then sent to attack mutineers at Camp Redjaf, the mission of soldiers of the 6th Commando Battalion was to secure the city of Boma and disarm mutineers. (Author's collection)

General Dag Hammarskjöld,[25] the UN was in the process of weighing up the pros and cons of the so-called Tunisian Resolution whereby the organisation's Security Council would call upon Belgium to withdraw its troops and authorise its Secretary-General to take the necessary measures to do so. Assistance, provided through the United Nations Operations in the Congo (UNOC), would be given until Congolese national security forces were able to maintain order.[26] What the UN, itself, failed to understand at the time is that the inclusion of this condition was unrealistic in view of the shambolic state of the ANC. Still, on 15 July,

in any future negotiations with Tshombe. Then, seemingly unaware that his actions would exacerbate already delicate East–West relations, Lumumba's next mistake was to call on the Soviet Union for assistance to remove Belgian military forces.[24] Thankfully, by 14 July, and despite a series of heated discussions with UN Secretary-

UN Resolution 143 saw the first of 20,000 peacekeepers arrive in the Congo. By 25 July, 8,000 Tunisian, Moroccan, Swedish, Liberian, Irish, Ethiopian, Guinean and Ghanaian peacekeepers had been assigned to the mission and by 31 July they numbered over 11,000.[27] Eighty US C-130 Hercules turboprops, Military Air Transport

The T-6 4KA serial-numbered H-202 was hit by shrapnel during Operation Mangrove. Crash-landing on its way back to Matadi-Tshimpi airfield, its pilot Guy De Pijpere was injured but rescued by Belgian forces. (Daniel Brackx)

Service (MATS) C-124 Globemasters and 10 DC-3s were involved in transporting these troops.[28] These aircraft also participated in Operation New Tape and Operation SAFARI: the largest United States Air Force (USAF) airlifts since the Berlin blockade of 1948–1949. Both the 322nd and 1602nd Air Divisions based at Evreux-Fauville, and Chateauroux in France took part. They airlifted over 1,000 tons of food and over 2,500 refugees.[29] Soviet planes were also used in the transport of troops. Five Ilyushin-II-12 turboprops carried in food donated by the USSR, and they transported Ghanaian troops from Accra to Léopoldville.[30]

Back in Belgium, Minister

Belgian army officer Major Guy Weber (left) was appointed chief military advisor to Tshombe while another, Jean-Marie Crèvecoeur, became the commander of the Katangese Gendarmes. (Albert Grandolini)

of Defence Gilson was acutely of the difficulties faced by Cométro commander General Gheysen. Convening a meeting of the Belgian joint chiefs of staff, and to ensure the safety of Europeans in the Congo it was then decided that its chairman Lieutenant General Charles Paul de Cumont would be sent to the former colony to replace Gheysen. Departing from Zaventem and arriving at BAKA on 13 July, De Cumont's first action was to authorise its commander Colonel Remy Van Lierde to send Belgian troops to Albertville (now Kalemie), Kolwezi, Kabalo and Kongolo. While the Second World War fighter ace was only too willing to execute these orders, De Cumont travelled to Luano where he was warmly greeted by Moïse Tshombe. At a following press conference, Du Cumont announced that Belgium had promised to lend support to Katanga's secession and would assist Tshombe in maintaining public order and setting up institutions of state. Belgian Prime Minister Pierre Wigny then

appointing Count Harold d'Aspremont Lynden to head the Belgian Technical Delegation (MISTEBEL) from 22 July 1960,[31] De Cumont appointed Major Jean-Marie Crèvecoeur as commander of the newly created Katangese army and Commandant Guy Weber as military advisor to Tshombe. This new Belgian-backed military force in the Congo was named the Katangese Gendarmes, and unofficial channels brought hundreds of Belgian ex-servicemen to Katanga to fight for Katanga's cause and to defend Belgian nationals. Forming the so-called Tshombe Brigade and comprising members of the *Comité d'action et de défense des Belges d'Afrique* (CABDA) and the *Corps Franc Roi Baudouin* (CFRB) that began to arrive in July 1960, this month would also see the creation of the Katangese Air Force (FAK) commanded by Belgian pilot Victor Volant and including Belgian pilots Joseph Delin and José Magain.

Former Belgian servicemen volunteered to join Katangan armed forces. Here, Moïse Tshombe shows his appreciation for their service. (Albert Grandolini)

of Paratroopers were sent to intervene when Congolese soldiers held several Europeans hostage. These operations ending in success for Belgian forces, they coincided with the aforementioned operations at Ndjili Airport. In this case, the intervention of Belgian troops related to De Cumont's strategy of systematically taking control of airfields and airports.[33] On 13 July, then, he authorised Gheysen to occupy Ndjili and to free it from Congolese mutineers. Operations began at dawn when commandos based at Camp Stanley began their approach towards the airport. Provided with air cover from Harvards and supported by

As the recruitment of Belgian mercenaries got under way in cafés dotted around Brussels, and although hundreds of ANC switched allegiance to Tshombe, in Jadotville some of his still-mutinous opponents based at Camp Bia were resisting all attempts to force their surrender. Their refusal to lay down their weapons continuing until 13 July, ending their occupation of the camp required the intervention of Belgian paracommandos flown from Belgium to BAKA on 9 July. Then dropped by four Fairchild C-119Cs over Kabalo, these men of the 11th Company were transported in civilian vehicles requisitioned for the purpose, and supported by the FAF, the standoff at Bia concluded when the 1,400 mutineers surrendered.[32] Other operations involving Belgian forces took place in the towns of Manono in northern Katanga, and at Bakwanga in the Kasai. Both mining centres, three units of the 13th Company

paratroopers, in all it took an hour to disarm the rebellious soldiers. Again using the 15th Transport Wing, Belgian troops of the 5th Commando Battalion and of the 14th Independent Company of Parachutists then secured the perimeters of the aerodrome. As soon as this task had been accomplished, Belgian airlines SABENA and Sobelair restarted the repatriation of Europeans towards Europe. Other airlines that took part in the evacuation were Lufthansa, KLM, and Air France. Then, as Kamina was considered too far from the Congolese, Gheysens made Ndjili his HQ and directed operations from the control tower.

16 July 1960 saw the transfer of four 4KAs and five pilots to Ndjili (Michel de Temmerman, André Gilles, Frank Swietek, Frans Allaeys and Henri Bernier), now bringing the number of 4KAs in Léopoldville to nine (H-22, H-23, H-34, H-35, H-207, H-210,

Belgian paratroopers at Ndjili Airport on 13 July 1960. These troops were sent to assist in the evacuation of Belgian citizens from the capital. Behind them is a Boeing 707 operated by SABENA. (Albert Grandolini)

A Belgian paratrooper secures the restaurant terrasse at Ndjili on 13 July 1960. (Author's collection)

18 was to provide air cover between the capital and Matadi, and to escort aircraft operated by the Avimil when carrying out rescue operations. Under the command of Major Avi Eric 'Toto' Bouzin, the position of the Avimil was somewhat confused since the Africanisation of the Congo's armed forces and the creation of the ANC. However, through the rescue missions it was able to find some form of identity, and its Alouette IIs (A-51 and A-52) plus a Sikorsky H-19 were put to good use at Kimpese in the Luozi territory on 15 July to rescue and evacuate protestant missionaries caught up in local violence exacted by Congolese soldiers.[34]

The joint rescue operations involving the BAF and the Avimil continuing until 17 July 1960, Belgium's military

H-213, H-216, and H-220). Belgian commanders fearing that mutineers may attempt to retake Ndjili, the early afternoon also saw the arrival of a detachment of six armed Potez-Air Fouga CM.170-1 Magisters. Operating alongside the Harvards of the FAF, the role of Fougas numbered MT-4, MT-6, MT-10, MT-14, MT-17 and MT- operations in the Congo and those of the soon-to-be defunct air wing of the FP were drawing to a conclusion as the UN applied pressure on the Belgian government to withdraw its troops. Generals De Cumont and Gheysen met with General Henry Templer Alexander (Ghana) and General Carl Von Horn (Sweden) of the UN in

A detachment of six Potez-Air Fouga CM.170-1 Magisters also arrived on the same day. Here, MT-6 is pictured at Ndjili. A USAF C-130 can be seen in the background. (Daniel Brackx)

Léopoldville on 17, 18 and 19 July, and it was agreed that Belgian troops would leave the Congo on 23 July at 1800. As a consequence of this agreement, five Fairchild C-119Gs and other transport aircraft were sent from BAKA to retrieve Belgian troops where they would meet up with the FAF Hravards, the Fouga Magisters and the aircraft of the Avimil. However, rescue operations continued in the Kindu province and in Katanga. In the latter instance, the FAF was used to persuade mutinous ANC troops based at Nzilo to hand over 40mm Bofors and heavy machine guns to Katangese authorities. Based temporarily at Kolwezi in an operation known as "Simba Red", aircraft of the FAF fired rockets at enemy positions while ground troops advanced towards these positions on foot. This operation resulting in the death of two Belgian soldiers and 13 mutineers, Belgian aircraft were then used to assist Katangese authorities in protecting Katanga's borders from attack by ANC soldiers. This military cooperation between Belgium and Katanga a sign of things to come, the evacuation of Belgium's military bases in the Congo continued throughout early August 1960. On 6 August, the Naval Task Group left Banana and headed back to Ostend, while on 8 August the UN Security Council requested that Belgium withdraw its troops from Katanga immediately.

As BAKA and other Belgian air bases in the Congo were gradually taken over by UNOC forces, most of the aircraft used by Belgian forces were taken to Ruanda-Urundi. As for those used by the Avi/FP, they had a different destiny in that they would form the basis of the Avikat, or Katangan Air Force. Its DH Heron, six DH Doves, one Sikorsky, two Alouette IIs officially became part of Tshombe's forces on 23 August as well as two of the BAF's C-47 Dakotas (K-19 became KAT-03, and K-21 became KAT-02). As for the Fouga CM.170s, some were disassembled and taken by Fairchild C-119G to Rhodesia before being taken to South Africa and back to Belgium. Lastly, and in some respects similar to Belgian presence in the Congo, the T-6s used by the FAF knew a rather undignified ending. Indeed, whereas H-15, H-19, H-216 and H-223 were sold to South Africa in January 1961 from their base in Usumbura, 13 others that were left at BAKA were destroyed on the orders of the UNOC. Though still in working order, the fuselages of these aircraft were shunted into the Congolese countryside by bulldozers and the wings were attacked by Congolese soldiers using pickaxes.[35] This incident took place on 27 January 1961, 10 days after Lumumba was assassinated in Katanga; an occurrence that added fuel to an already explosive situation in the Congo, and one that would see the country torn apart by years of civil war. During these years of armed strife, Belgian forces would return in the shape of the *Force Aérienne Tactique Congo* (FATAC), the subject of volume 2 of this series.

Bibliography

Monographs

Abbott, Peter, *Armies in East Africa* (Oxford: Osprey Publishing, 2002)

Akeampong, Emmanuel Kwaku and Gates, Henry Louis, *Dictionary of African Biography* (New York: OUP, 2012)

Bethune, Arm, *Le Katanga, Province Belge,* (Paris: Broché, 2010)

Brackx, Daniel, Sonck, Jean-Pierre, *L'appui-feu de Baka* (Editions De Krijger, 2008)

Brausch, Georges, *Belgian Administration in the Congo* (Oxford, OUP, 1961)

Burghardt Du Bois, William Edward, "Fifth Pan-African Congress final resolution", October 1945, W. E. B. Du Bois Papers (MS 312). Special Collections and University Archives, University of Massachusetts Amherst Libraries

Charles de Kavanagh Boulger, Demetrius, *The Congo State* (London: Thacker & Co., 1895)

Charles, Jean-Léon, *Les forces armées belges au cours de la Deuxième guerre mondiale, 1940–1945* (Brussels: Renaissance du livre, 1970)

Chrétien, Jean-Pierre, *Burundi, l'histoire retrouvée: 25 ans de métier d'historien en Afrique* (Paris: Karthala, 1993)

Cornet, René, *La bataille du rail* (Brussels: Editions L. Cuypers, 1953) p.336, in Verhaegen, *ABAKO: 1950–1960* (Brussels: CRISP, 1962)

Crawford, Daniel, *Thinking Black: 22 Years without a Break in the Long Grass* (George H. Doran: New York, 1912)

Devlin, Lawrence, *Chief of Station, Congo* (New York: Public Affairs, 2008)

Luc De Vos, Luc, Gérard-Libois, Jules and Raxhorn, Philippe, *Les secrets de l'affaire Lumumba* (Bruxelles: Editions Racine, 2005)

Edgerton, Robert B., *The Troubled Heart of Africa* (New York: St. Martin's Press, 2002)

Farwell, Byron, *The Great War in Africa, 1914 – 1918* (New York, W.W. Norton & Company, 1989)

Fox Bourne, Henry Richard, *Civilisation in Congoland, a Story of International Wrong-Doing* (London: P.S King & son, 1903)

Gann, Lewis H. and Duignan, Peter, *The Rulers of Belgian Africa, 1884–1914* (Princeton: Princeton University Press, 1979)

Gerard, Emmanuel and Kulick, Bruce, *Death in the Congo: Murdering Patrice Lumumba* (Cambridge, Mass., Harvard University Press, 2015)

Hempstone, Smith, *Rebels, Mercenaries, and Dividends – the Katanga Story* (New York: Fredrick Praeger, 1962)

Hinde, Sidney Langford, *The Fall of the Congo Arabs* (London: Methuen, 1897)

Hochschild, Adam, *King Leopold's Ghost: A Story of Greed, Terrorism and Heroism in Colonial Africa* (Boston & New York: Houghton Mifflin Company, 1998)

Hordern, Charles, *Military Operations in East Africa, Volume 1, August 1914 – September 1916* (London: HMSO, 1941)

Foden, Giles, *Mimi and Toutou Go Forth: The Bizarre Battle for Lake Tanganyika* (London: Penguin, 2005)

Haskin, Jeanne M., *The Tragic State of the Congo: from Decolonization to Dictatorship* (New York: Algora Publishing, 2005)

Kalb, Madeleine, *The Congo Cables: The Cold War in Africa – From Eisenhower to Kennedy* (London: Macmillan, 1982)

Kantowitz, Edward R., *The World in the Twentieth Century Vol.2: Coming Apart, Coming Together* (Cambridge: William B. Eerdmans Publishing Company, 2000)

Kryza, Frank T., *The Race for Timbuktu: In Search of Africa's City of Gold* (New York: Harper Collins, 2006)

Legum, Colin, *Congo Disaster* (Baltimore: Penguin Books, 1960)

Livingstone, David, *The Last Journals of David Livingstone in Central Africa* (New York: Harper and Brothers Limited, 1875)

Murindwa-Rutanga, *Politics, Religion and Power in the Great Lakes Region* (Fountain Publishers: Kampala, 2011)

Ndongala Mumbata, Didier, *Patrice Lumumba, Ahead of His Time* (London: Paragon Publishing, 2018)

Nzongola-Ntalaja, Georges, *From Leopold to Kabila: A People's History* (London: Zed Books, 2002)

Oliver, Roland and Atmore, Anthony, *Medieval Africa, 1250–1800* (Cambridge: Cambridge University Press, 2001)

Paice, Edward, *Tip & Run: The Untold Tragedy of the Great War in Africa* (London: Phoenix, 2008)

Rookes, Stephen, *Ripe for Rebellion: Political and Military Insurgency in the Congo, 1946–1964* (Warwick: Helion & Co., 2021)

Rookes, Stephen, *For God and the CIA: Cuban Exile Military Operations in the Congo and Beyond, 1959–1967* (Warwick: Helion & Co., 2021)

Samarin, William J., *The Black Man's Burden: African Colonial Labor on the Congo and Ubangi Rivers, 1880–1900* (Boulder: Westview Press, 1989)

Smith, Norman, *The British Commonwealth Air Training Plan* (Toronto: Macmillan, 1941)

Soret, Marcel, *Les Kongo Nord-Occidentaux* (Paris: L'Harmattan, 1959)

Stapleton, Timothy J., *A Military History of Africa (3 volumes)* (ABC-CLIO, 2013)

Stiénon, Charles, *La Campagne Anglo-Belge de L'Afrique Orientale Allemande* (Paris: Nabu Press, 2011)

Thomas, Martin, *Violence and Colonial Order: Police, Workers and Protest in the European Colonial Empires, 1918–1940* (Cambridge: Cambridge University Press, 2012)

Van Bilsen, A.A. J., *Vers l'indépendance du Congo et du Ruanda-Urundi* (Kinshasa: Presses Universitaires, 1977)

Van Crombrugge, Colonel A. «Aviation in the Belgian Congo», from «Premier Congrès International de la Navigation Aérienne», Paris, November 1921

Guy Vanthemsche, *La Belgique et le Congo: Empreintes d'une colonie, 1885–1980* (Brussels: Complexe, 2007)

Vanthemsche, Guy, *Belgium and the Congo, 1885–1990* (Cambridge: Cambridge University Press, 2012)

Veranneman, Jean-Michel, *Belgium in the Second World War* (Barnsley: Pen & Sword, 2014)

Verhaegen, Benoît, *L'ABAKO et l'indépendance du Congo belge: dix ans de nationalisme kongo* (Paris: L'Harmattan, 2003)

Verhaegen, Benoît, *ABAKO, 1950–1960* (Brussels: Documents du CRISP, 1962)

Wack, Henry Wellington, *The Story of the Congo Free State: Social, Political and Economic Aspects of the Belgian System of Government in Central Africa* (New York & London: G.P. Putnam's Sons, 1905)

Weller, George, "The Belgian Campaign in Ethiopia: A Trek of 2,500 Miles Through Jungle Swamps and Desert Wastes", Belgian Information Centre, New York, reprinted through the courtesy of The Chicago Daily News, 1941

Winterbottom, Harold St. John Lloyd *et al.*, *The Belgian Congo* (Great Britain: Naval Intelligence Division, 1944)

Young, Crawford, *Politics in the Congo: Decolonization and Independence* (Oxford: OUP, 1965)

Zeilig, Leo, Renton, David, and Seddon, David, *The Congo: Plunder and Resistance* (London: Zed Books, 2007)

Zeilig, Leo, *Lumumba: Africa's Lost Leader* (London: Haus, 2008)

Articles Published in Journals

Alcock, Rutherford, "African Exploration Fund", *Proceedings of the Royal Geographical Society of London*, Vol.21, No.6, 1876–1877

Calkins, Kenneth L., "Boeing's Flying Boat: A Great Adventure in Aviation and a Unique Chapter in Air Transportation History", *The Magazine of Northwest History*, Vol.17, No.2, Summer 2003

Coquilhat, Camille, *Sur le Haut Congo* (Brussels and Paris: J. Lebégue & Co., 1888)

Covington-Ward, Yolanda, "Joseph Kasa-Vubu, ABAKO? and Performances of Kongo Nationalism in the Independence of Congo", *Journal of Black Studies*, Special issue: 1960s Africa in Historical Perspective, Vol.43, No.1, January 2012

Heywood, Linda "Slavery and its Transformation in the Kingdom of the Kongo: 1491–1800", *The Journal of African History*, Vol.50, No.1

Houser, George M., "A Report on the All-African People's Conference Held in Accra, Ghana, December 8–13, 1958", *American Committee on Africa*, New York, 1961

Jewsiewicki, Bogumil, Lema, Kikola, Vellut, Jean-Luc, «Documents pour servir de l'histoire sociale du Zaïre: grèves dans le Bas-Congo en 1945», *Etudes d'histoire africaine*, 1973

Labrique, Jean, *Congo politique* (Léopoldville: Editions de l'Avenir, 1957)

Legum, Colin, "The Belgian Congo: Revolt of the Elite", *Africa South*, Vol.4, No.1, October-December 1959

Lemarchand, René, "The Bases of Nationalism among the Bakongo", *Africa: Journal of the International African Institute*, Vol.31, No.4, October 1961

Phillips, Henry Jnr., "An Account of the Congo Independent State", *Proceedings of the American Philosophical Society*, Vol.26, No.130, July – December 1889

Rubbens, A., "Political Awakening in the Congo", *Civilisations*, Vol.10, No.1, 1960

Slade, Ruth M., "King Leopold's Congo: Aspects of the Development of Race Relations in the Congo Independent State", *Institute of Race Relations* (Oxford, OUP, 1962)

Stenger, Jean, "The Congo Free State and the Congo before 1914" in Gavin, L.H. & Duigan, P., (eds.), *Colonialism in Africa* (Cambridge: Cambridge University Press, 1969)

Vanthemsche, Guy, "The Birth of Commercial Air Transport in Belgium (1919–1923)", *Revue belge de Philogie et d'Histoire*, 78-3-4, 2000

Young, Crawford, "Background to Independence", *Transition*, No.25, 1966

Governmental/Organisation Sources

Académie Royale des Sciences d'Outre-mer, «Tshombe, Moïse-Kapenda», *Biographie Belge d'Outre-Mer*, Brussels: Académie Royale des Sciences d'Outre-mer, (Tome VII-A)

International Labour Office, «Les problèmes du travail en Afrique» (Geneva: International Labour Office, 1959)

Institut Royal Colonial Belge, «La Force Publique de sa naissance à 1914», Ouvrage réalisé par la Deuxième Section de l'Etat-major de la Force Publique, 1952

Institut Royal Colonial Belge, «Hanssens, Edmond Winnie Victor», *Biographie Coloniale Belge*, T.I., 1948

Institut Royale de la colonie belge, «Louis Marie François Frank», *Biographie Coloniale Belge*, Tome III, 1952

Institut Royal Colonial Belge - Atlas général du Congo / Algemene atlas van Congo (in fr, nl), Belgium: Institut Royal Colonial Belge, 1948–1963

Articles from Digital Sources

"Aerial Visuals, Airframe Dossier", <https://www.aerialvisuals.ca/AirframeDossier.php?Serial=96250>, accessed 24 September 2021

"Aircraft G-BSGC Data", <https://www.airport-data.com/aircraft/G-BSGC.html>, accessed 24 September 2021

"AS.10 Oxford For Export", <http://britishaviation-ptp.com/airspeed_as10.html>, accessed 22 September 2021

"Airspeed AS.65 Consul", <http://britishaviation-ptp.com/airspeed_as65.html>, accessed 19 September 2021

"Airspeed Oxford", <https://www.belgian-wings.be/airspeed-oxford-i>, accessed 20 September 2021

Badou, Luc, «Les avions de la Force Publique du Congo», <http://web.archive.org/web/20121212013530/http://www.likasi.be/Avions/de Force Publique/duCongo.htm> accessed 19 September 2021

"Belgian Congo (1908–1960)", <https://uca.edu/politicalscience/dadm-project/sub-saharan-africa-region/belgian-congo-1908-1960/>, accessed 15 August 2021

Brion, R. and Moreau, J-L., *De la mine à Mars: La Genèse d'Umicore*, (Brussels: Lannoo, 2006), p.69 as quoted in «Les Géants du Cuivre: Leçons tirées des Entreprises Etatiques Minières en RDC et en Zambie», *Natural Resource Governance Institute*, undated, p.15, https://www.resourcegovernance.org/sites/default/files/documents/nrgi_nmc_french.pdf, accessed 12 June 2021

"Bristol 171 Sycamore HR.14B", < https://www.belgian-wings.be/bristol-171-sycamore-hr-14b>, accessed 19 September 2021

Buzin, Jean, "The Belgian Congo Air Force": the Air Force that Never was", https://www.vieillestiges.be/files/articles/belgiancongoairforce_fr.pdf, accessed 20 July 2021

"Caudron Pélican", <https://www.belgian-wings.be/caudron-c510-pelican> accessed 20 September 2021

"Caudron Super Phalène", <https://www.belgian-wings.be/caudron-super-phalène>, accessed 20 September 2021

"Civil Aircraft Register – Belgian Congo", <http://www.airhistory.org.uk/gy/reg_OO-.html> accessed 12 June 2021

"Clipper Capetown", <https://pan-american-clippers.fandom.com/wiki/Clipper_Capetown>, accessed 12 June 2021

De Coster, Pieter, "Biografie van Paul le Marinel", De eerste Europese ontdekkingsreizen in Katanga, 1797–1897, <http://www.ethesis.net/katanga/katanga_hfst_7.htm#blad13>, accessed 25 July 2021

Dillien, André, «Régistre 9O-9Q-9T-KAT», <https://doczz.fr/doc/71037/liste-des-immatriculations>, accessed 24 September 2021

Ergo, André-Bernard, "Congo belge 1914–1918", <http://abergo1.e-monsite.com/medias/files/cb-14-18-guerre-est-allemand.pdf>, accessed 03/08/2021

"From a letter to Dag Hammarskjöld, U.N. Secretary-General, August 14, 1960", https://www.marxists.org/subject/africa/lumumba/1960/08/umgensec.htm, accessed 19 October 2021

Haulman, Daniel L., "Congolese Mercy Airlift", *Air Mobility Command Museum*, (date unknown) available at <https://amcmuseum.org/history/congolese-mercy-airlift/>, accessed 1 July 2019

"Junkers Ju52/3m", <https://www.belgian-wings.be/junkers-ju52-3m>, accessed 22 September 2021

"Kinshasa Then and Now", 27 April 2013, <http://kosubaawate. blogspot.com/2013/04/1925-ndolo-airport-first-flight-from.html>, accessed 12 June 2021

«La Force Publique congolaise», *Mémoires du Congo*, No.38, juin 2016, https://www.memoiresducongo.be/wp-content/uploads/2016/09/ MDC-38.pdf, accessed 14 June 2021

"Leopoldville 1942 – U.S. Troops Upgrade Ndolo Airport", 23 May 2011, <http://kosubaawate.blogspot.com/2011/05/leopoldville-1942-us-troops-expand.html>, accessed 13 June 2021

«Les avions de la Force Publique du Congo», <https://www. belgian-wings.be/de-havilland-dh-104-dove/d-14>, accessed 24 September 2021

"Les Belges dans la South African Air Force, 1940–1944", https://www. vieillestiges.be/fr/articles/18, accessed 25 August 2021

Lumumba, Patrice, "Speech at Accra", <https://www.blackpast.org/ global-african-history/1958-patrice-lumumba-speech-accra/> accessed 14 May 2021

"North American AT-6 Harvard/Texan", <https://www.belgian-wings. be/harvard-part-iv>, accessed 20 September 2021

"OO-AMN", <https://www.belgian-wings.be/de-havilland-dh-80-puss-moth/(oo-amn)>, accessed 22 September 2021

"SABENA World Airlines", <http://www.sabena.com/nl/history>, accessed 15/07/2021

Sonck, Jean-Pierre, «Les hydavions belges du Tanganyika», *Belgian Aviation History Association*, 2003, <https://www.albertville.be/ escadrille-tanganyika-01.html>, accessed 3 August 2021

Sonck, Jean-Pierre, "L'Aviation Légère", < https://www. memoiresducongo.be/wp-content/uploads/2020/04/MDC-52.pdf>, accessed 4 October 2021

"Stampe Vertongen SV-4B (Pre-War)", <https://www.belgian-wings.be/ stampe-vertongen-sv-4b-pre-war>, accessed 24 September 2021

"The Early Days", https://www.brusselsairport.be/en/our-airport/ about-brussels-airport/history/the-early-days, accessed 15 July 2021

"The Right Arm of the Free World: A Look into the History of the FN FAL", <https://www.itstactical.com/warcom/firearms/right-arm-free-world-look-history-fn-fal/>, accessed 25 September 2021

Doctoral Theses

Allen, Jr., Robert W., "Britain and Belgian Exiles, 1940–1945", PhD Thesis, University College, London, 1997

Shaw, Bryant P., "Force Publique, Force Unique: The Military in the Belgian Congo, 1914–1939", PhD Thesis presented at the University of Wisconsin-Madison, 1984

Newspaper Articles (by date)

Bigart, Homer, "Lumumba Victor in Congo Voting", *New York Times*, 1 June 1960

"Rhodesia to Bolster Border", *New York Times*, 1 June 1960

"Belgian Congo Threats Spur European's Exodus", *New York Times*, 2 June 1960

"Emergency Declared in Katanga", *The Times*, 14 June 1960

Gilroy, Harry, "Divisive Efforts Spread in Congo", *New York Times*, 14 June 1960

"Army to be Commanded by Congolese", *The Times*, 9 July 1960

"New Congo State to Enforce Unity", *The Times*, 28 June 1960

"Excerpts from Prof. Van Bilsen's "Thirty Year Plan", in "Conflict in the Congo", *Africa Today*, Vol.7, No.5, September 1960

Notes

Chapter 1

1 Linda Heywood, "Slavery and its Transformation in the Kingdom of the Kongo: 1491–1800", *The Journal of African History*, Vol.50, No.1, p.13.

2 Roland Oliver and Anthony Atmore, *Medieval Africa, 1250–1800* (Cambridge: Cambridge University Press, 2001), p.173.

3 Marcel Soret, *Les Kongo Nord-Occidentaux* (Paris: L'Harmattan, 1959), p.21, in Verhaegen, L'ABAKO et l'indépendance du Congo belge: dix ans de nationalisme kongo (Paris: L'Harmattan, 2003), p.19.

4 Frank T. Kryza, *The Race for Timbuktu: In Search of Africa's City of Gold* (New York: Harper Collins, 2006), p.11.

5 David Livingstone, *The Last Journals of David Livingstone in Central Africa* (New York: Harper and Brothers Limited, 1875).

6 Daniel Crawford, *Thinking Black: 22 Years without a Break in the Long Grass* (George H. Doran: New York, 1912), p.15.

7 Arm Bethune, *Le Katanga, Province Belge* (Paris: Broché, 2010), p.72.

8 Situated between the Democratic Republic of the Congo and Zambia.

9 Rutherford Alcock, "African Exploration Fund", *Proceedings of the Royal Geographical Society of London*, Vol.21, No.6, 1876–1877, pp.601–615.

10 Henry Phillips, Jnr., "An Account of the Congo Independent State", *Proceedings of the American Philosophical Society*, Vol.26, No.130, July – December 1889, pp.459–476.

11 Phillips, *An Account of the Congo Independent State*, p.460.

12 Edmond Winnie Victor Hanssens, "Biographie Coloniale Belge", *Institut Royal Colonial Belge*, T.I., 1948, Col. 479–493.

13 Pieter De Coster, "Biografie van Paul le Marinel", De eerste Europese ontdekkingsreizen in Katanga, 1797–1897, available at http://www.ethesis.net/katanga/katanga_hfst_7.htm#blad13, accessed 10/05/2021.

14 "La Force Publique de sa naissance à 1914", Ouvrage réalisé par la Deuxième Section de l'Etat-major de la Force Publique, *Institut Royal Colonial Belge*, 1952, p.10.

15 *La Force Publique de sa naissance à 1914*, p.11.

16 Camille Coquilhat, *Sur le Haut Congo* (Brussels and Paris: J. Lebégue & Co., 1888), p.228.

17 *La Force Publique de sa naissance à 1914*, p.17.

18 Table adapted from *La Force Publique de sa naissance à 1914*, p.513.

19 Table adapted from *La Force Publique de sa naissance à 1914*, p.506.

20 Lewis H. Gann, and Peter Duignan, *The Rulers of Belgian Africa, 1884–1914* (Princeton: Princeton University Press, 1979), p.60.

21 Table adapted from *La Force Publique de sa naissance à 1914*, p.509.

22 Table adapted from *La Force Publique de sa naissance à 1914*, p.505.

23 Bryant P. Shaw, "Force Publique, Force Unique: The Military in the Belgian Congo, 1914–1939", PhD Thesis presented at the University of Wisconsin-Madison, 1984, p.12.

24 The three Governor-Generals of the CFS were Francis de Winton, 1884–1886, Camille Jannsen, 1886–1887, and Théophile Wahis, 1892–1908. Francis de Winton was a British Army officer and secretary to the Marquess of Lorne, the Governor General of Canada.

25 Bulletin Officiel (BO), 1885, p.25, in Shaw, *Force Publique, Force Unique: The Military in the Belgian Congo, 1914–1939*, p.12.

26 Bulletin Officiel, 1888, p.251, in Shaw, *Force Publique, Force Unique: The Military in the Belgian Congo, 1914–1939*, p.12.

27 "Etude sur la Force Publique de l'Etat Indépendant du Congo", Brussels, 1895, pp.33–35 in Shaw, *Force Publique, Force Unique: The Military in the Belgian Congo, 1914–1939*, p.12.

28 Adapted from *La Force Publique de sa naissance à 1914*, p.516.

Chapter 2

1   "La Force Publique congolaise", *Mémoires du Congo*, No.38, juin 2016, p.4. Another source puts the number of men in the FP at 19,000 by 1900. See, Adam Hochschild, *King Leopold's Ghost: A Story of Greed, Terrorism and Heroism in Colonial Africa* (Boston & New York: Houghton Mifflin Company, 1998), p.115.

2   Henry Wellington Wack, *The Story of the Congo Free State: Social, Political and Economic Aspects of the Belgian System of Government in Central Africa* (New York & London, G.P. Putnam's Sons, 1905), pp.177–182.

3   Sidney Langford Hinde, *The Fall of the Congo Arabs* (London: Methuen, 1897), p.33 in Robert B. Edgerton, *The Troubled Heart of Africa* (New York: St. Martin's Press, 2002), pp.100–101.

4   Jean-Pierre Chrétien, *Burundi, l'histoire retrouvée: 25 ans de métier d'historien en Afrique* (Paris: Karthala, 1993), p.134.

5   Edgerton, *The Troubled Heart of Africa*, p.104.

6   Demetrius Charles de Kavanagh Boulger, *The Congo State* (London: Thacker & Co., 1895), p.180.

7   Adapted from *La Force Publique de sa naissance à 1914*, p.521.

8   Wack, *The Story of the Congo Free State*, p.217.

9   S.J. Stenger, "The Congo free State and the Congo before 1910", in L.H. Gavin & P. Duigan (eds.), *Colonialism in Africa* (Cambridge: Cambridge University Press, 1969), p.227.

10 Wack, *The Story of the Congo Free State*, p.220.

11 "The Story of Congo Free State", pp.220–221.

12 Crawford Young, *Politics in the Congo: Decolonization and Independence* (Oxford: OUP, 1965), p.441.

13 Adapted from "La Force Publique de sa naissance à 1914", p.524.

14 Adapted from *La Force Publique de sa naissance à 1914*, p.526.

15 Hochschild, *King Leopold's Ghost*, pp.127–128.

16 Adapted from *La Force Publique de sa naissance à 1914*, p.528.

17 Smith Hempstone, *Rebels, Mercenaries, and Dividends – the Katanga Story* (New York: Fredrick Praeger, 1962), p.13.

18 Indeed, the practice doubtless inspired an episode of Joseph Conrad's novella *Heart of Darkness* (1899). Conrad describes how a Belgian trader named Kurtz has become imbibed with the conditions in the Congo, and how his heart moved over to the dark side. Kurtz also places heads on stakes around his encampment as does his namesake in Francis Ford Coppola's war epic *Apocalypse Now*.

19 Hempstone, *Rebels, Mercenaries and Dividends – the Katanga Story*, p.19.

20 Hempstone, *Rebels, Mercenaries and Dividends – the Katanga Story*, p.14.

21 Hempstone, *Rebels, Mercenaries and Dividends – the Katanga Story*, p.18.

22 Hempstone, *Rebels, Mercenaries and Dividends – the Katanga Story*, p.19.

23 Adapted from *La Force Publique de sa naissance à 1914*, p.520.

24 R. Brion and J-L Moreau, *De la mine à Mars: La Genèse d'Umicore* (Brussels: Lannoo, 2006), p.69 as quoted in "Les Géants du Cuivre: Leçons tirées des Entreprises Etatiques Minières en RDC et en Zambie", *Natural Resource Governance Institute*, undated, p.15, https://www.resourcegovernance.org/sites/default/files/documents/nrgi_nmc_french.pdf, accessed September 2021.

25 William J. Samarin, *The Black Man's Burden: African Colonial Labor on the Congo and Ubangi Rivers, 1880–1900* (Boulder: Westview Press, 1989, p.119.

26 Leo Zeilig, David Renton, and David Seddon, *The Congo: Plunder and Resistance* (London: Zed Books, 2007), p.38.

27 Ruth M. Slade, "King Leopold's Congo: Aspects of the Development of Race Relations in the Congo Independent State", *Institute of Race Relations* (Oxford, OUP, 1962), p.177.

28 Harold St. John Lloyd Winterbottom, et al., *The Belgian Congo* (Great Britain: Naval Intelligence Division, 1944), p.200.

29 Henry Richard Fox Bourne, *Civilisation in Congoland, a Story of International Wrong-Doing* (London: P.S King & son, 1903), p.89.

30 Winterbottom, et al., *The Belgian Congo*, p.207.

31 René Cornet, *La bataille du rail* (Brussels: Editions L. Cuypers, 1953) p.336, in Verhaegen, *ABAKO: 1950–1960* (Brussels: CRISP, 1962), p.20

Chapter 3

1   Peter Abbott, *Armies in East Africa* (Oxford: Osprey Publishing, 2002), p.9.

2   Murindwa-Rutanga, *Politics, Religion and Power in the Great Lakes Region* (Fountain Publishers: Kampala, 2011), p.87.

3   Abbott, *Armies in East Africa*, p.9.

4   Abbott, *Armies in East Africa*, p.9.

5   Charles Hordern, *Military Operations in East Africa, Volume 1, August 1914 – September 1916* (London: HMSO, 1941), p.49.

6   Hordern, *Military Operations in East Africa*, p.50.

7   Byron Farwell, *The Great War in Africa, 1914 – 1918* (New York, W.W. Norton & Company, 1989), p.178.

8   Hordern, *Military Operations in East Africa*, p.177.

9   Hordern, *Military Operations in East Africa*, p.178.

10 Hordern, *Military Operations in East Africa*, p.183.

11 André-Bernard Ergo, "Congo belge 1914–1918", <http://abergo1.e-monsite.com/medias/files/cb-14-18-guerre-est-allemand.pdf>, accessed 03/08/2021.

12 For more on this episode see, Giles Foden, *Mimi and Toutou Go Forth: The Bizarre Battle for Lake Tanganyika* (London: Penguin, 2005).

13 J-P Sonck, "Les hydravions belges du Tanganyika", *Belgian Aviation History Association*, 2003, https://www.albertville.be/escadrille-tanganyika-01.html, accessed 03/08/2021.

14 Sonck, *Les hydravions belges du Tanganyika*.

15 For more on mercenary operations in the Congo Crisis, see Stephen Rookes, *Ripe for Rebellion: Political and Military Insurgency in the Congo, 1946–1964* (Warwick: Helion & Co., 2021), and Stephen Rookes, *For God and the CIA: Cuban Exile Military Operations in the Congo and Beyond, 1959–1967* (Warwick: Helion & Co., 2021).

16 Sonck, *Les hydravions belges du Tanganyika*.

17 Hordern, *Military Operations in East Africa*, p.405.

18 Hordern, *Military Operations in East Africa*, p.406.

19 Hordern, *Military Operations in East Africa*, p.408.

20 Sonck, *Les hydravions belges du Tanganyika*.

21 *Paice, Tip & Run: The Untold Tragedy of the Great War in Africa*, p.230.

22 Hordern, *Military Operations in East Africa*, p.441.

23 Charles Stiénon, *La Campagne Anglo-Belge de L'Afrique Orientale Allemande* (Paris: Nabu Press, 2011), p.197.

24 "Force Publique", https://encyclopedia.1914-1918-online.net/article/force_publique>, accessed 06/08/2021.

25 Martin Thomas, *Violence and Colonial Order: Police, Workers and Protest in the European Colonial Empires, 1918–1940* (Cambridge: Cambridge University Press, 2012), p.305.

Chapter 4

1   Winterbottom, et al., *The Belgian Congo*, pp.240–241.

2   Winterbottom, et al., *The Belgian Congo*, pp.235.

3   "Louis Marie François Frank", *Biographie Coloniale Belge*, Institut Royale de la colonie belge, Tome III, 1952, pp.325–343.

4   Funds put at the disposal of the king for special projects in the Belgian Congo.

5   National Syndicate for the Study of Air Transport.

6   Colonel A. van Crombrugge, "Aviation in the Belgian Congo", from "Premier Congrès International de la Navigation Aérienne", Paris, November 1921, p.1.

7   Van Crombrugge, *Aviation in the Belgian Congo*", p.2.

8   Van Crombrugge, *Aviation in the Belgian Congo*, pp.5–6.

9   Guy Vanthemsche, "The Birth of Commercial Air Transport in Belgium (1919–1923)", *Revue belge de Philogie et d'Histoire*, 78-3-4, 2000, p.925.

10 "The Early Days", https://www.brusselsairport.be/en/our-airport/about-brussels-airport/history/the-early-days, accessed 15/07/2021.

11 Vanthemsche, *The Birth of Commercial Air Transport in Belgium (1919–1923)*, pp.913–944.

12 Winterbottom, et al., *The Belgian Congo*, pp.240–241.

13 "SABENA World Airlines", <http://www.sabena.com/nl/history>, accessed15/07/2021.

Chapter 5

1   For more on these aspects, see Shaw, *Force Publique, Force Unique...*, pp. 125–133.

2   O. Louwers, "Note pour M. le Ministre", 24 January 1922, AMAE, AF-I-i (1922), p.6, in Guy Vanthemsche, *Belgium and the Congo, 1885–1990* (Cambridge: Cambridge University Press, 2012), p.118.

3   Vanthemsche, *Belgium and the Congo, 1885–1990*, p.119.

4   Vanthemsche, *Belgium and the Congo, 1885–1990*, pp.122–123.

5   Vanthemsche, *Belgium and the Congo, 1885–1990*, p.124.

6   Vanthemsche, *Belgium and the Congo, 1885–1990*, p.126.

7   Vanthemsche, *Belgium and the Congo, 1885–1990*, p.126.

8   Jean-Michel Veranneman, *Belgium in the Second World War* (Barnsley: Pen & Sword, 2014), p.79.

9   Robert W. Allen, Jr., "Britain and Belgian Exiles, 1940–1945", PhD Thesis, University College, London, 1997, p.118.

10 "HQ W. Africa Forces Meeting", 5–6 August 1941.WO 103/2892: 14, in "Britain and Belgian Exiles, 1940–1945".

11 Jean-Léon Charles, *Les forces armées belges au cours de la Deuxième guerre mondiale, 1940–1945* (Brussels: Renaissance du livre, 1970), p.82.

12 George Weller, "The Belgian Campaign in Ethiopia: A Trek of 2,500 Miles Through Jungle Swamps and Desert Wastes", Belgian Information Centre, New York, reprinted through the courtesy of The Chicago Daily News, 1941.

13 Weller, *The Belgian Campaign in Ethiopia*, p.20.

14 Weller, *The Belgian Campaign in Ethiopia*, p.21.

15 Weller, *The Belgian Campaign in Ethiopia*, p.21.

16 Timothy J. Stapleton, *A Military History of Africa (3 volumes)* (ABC-CLIO, 2013), p.272.

17 The invasion of Dahomey was cancelled when it became controlled by Free French forces.

18 Stapleton, *A Military History of Africa*, pp.227–228.

Chapter 6

1   Jean Buzin, "The Belgian Congo Air Force": the Air Force that Never was", <https://www.vieillestiges.be/files/articles/belgiancongoairforce_fr.pdf,>, accessed 20/08/2021.

2   Buzin, *The Belgian Congo Air Force*": the Air Force that Never was*, pp.4–6.

3   Norman Smith, *The British Commonwealth Air Training Plan* (Toronto: Macmillan, 1941), p.9.

4   "Les Belges dans la South African Air Force, 1940–1944", <https://www.vieillestiges.be/fr/articles/18>, accessed 25/08/2021.

5   "Les Belges dans la South African Air Force, 1940–1944", p.6.

6   Buzin, *The Belgian Congo Air Force: The Air Force that Never was*, p.8.

7   "Kinshasa Then and Now", 27 April 2013, <http://kosubaawate.blogspot.com/2013/04/1925-ndolo-airport-first-flight-from.html>, accessed 12/09/2021.

8   Crashed 31 May 1943. Civil Aircraft Register – Belgium, <http://www.airhistory.org.uk/gy/reg_OO-.html>, accessed 12/09/2021.

9   Withdrawn from use January 1943. Civil Aircraft Register – Belgium.

10 Withdrawn from use 16 July 1945. Civil Aircraft Register – Belgium.

11 Withdrawn from use November 1944. Civil Aircraft Register – Belgium.

12 Damaged 31 May 1943, withdrawn from use 16 July 1945. Civil Aircraft Register – Belgium.

13 Withdrawn from use 16 July 1945. Civil Aircraft Register – Belgium.

14 Arriving in the Congo on 21 October 1938, it was sold on 22 October 1945. Civil Aircraft Register – Belgium.

15 Crashed Mongana, Congo 3 April 1944. Civil Aircraft Register – Belgium

16 Crashed Bangui 1 January 1943. Civil Aircraft Register – Belgium.

17 Sold 25 November 1946. Civil Aircraft Register – Belgium.

18 Adapted from "Civil Aircraft Register – Belgian Congo".

19 "Leopoldville 1942 – U.S. Troops Upgrade Ndolo Airport", 23 May 2011, <http://kosubaawate.blogspot.com/2011/05/leopoldville-1942-us-troops-expand.html>, accessed 13/09/2021.

20 Buzin, *The Belgian Congo Air Force: The Air Force that Never was*, p.12.

21 Buzin, *The Belgian Congo Air Force: The Air Force that Never was*, pp.13–14.

22 The WEA or the Treaty of Economic, Social and Cultural Collaboration and Collective Self-Defence was signed by Great Britain, France, Belgium, the Netherlands, and Luxembourg on 17 March 1948. It was created as East-Wast tensions mounted in Europe with the USSR seeking to impose its domination over central European countries.

23 Guy Vanthemsche, *La Belgique et le Congo : Empreintes d'une colonie, 1885–1980* (Brussels: Complexe, 2007), p.212.

24 Jean-Pierre Sonck, "L'Aviation Légère", < https://www.memoiresducongo.be/wp-content/uploads/2020/04/MDC-52.pdf>, accessed 4 October 2021.

25 See "Airspeed Oxford", <https://www.belgian-wings.be/airspeed-oxford-i>, accessed 20 September 2021.

26 See "AS.10 Oxford For Export", <http://britishaviation-ptp.com/airspeed_as10.html>, accessed 22 September 2021.

27 "Airspeed AS.65 Consul", <http://britishaviation-ptp.com/airspeed_as65.html>, accessed 19 September 2021.

28 "Bristol 171 Sycamore HR.14B", < https://www.belgian-wings.be/bristol-171-sycamore-hr-14b>, accessed 19 September 2021.

29 See "Caudron Pélican", <https://www.belgian-wings.be/caudron-super-phalène>, accessed 20 September 2021.

30 See "Cuadron Super Phalène", <https://www.belgian-wings.be/caudron-c510-pelican>, accessed 20 September 2021.

31 Luc Badou, "Les avions de la Force Publique du Congo", <http://web.archive.org/web/20121212013530/http://www.likasi.be/Avions/de Force Publique/duCongo.html>, accessed 19 September 2021.

32 "OO-AMN", <https://www.belgian-wings.be/de-havilland-dh-80-puss-moth/(oo-amn)>, accessed 22 September 2021.

33 Badou, Les avions de la Force Publique du Congo.

34 Data on this aircraft adapted from "Les avions de la Force Publique du Congo", <https://www.belgian-wings.be/de-havilland-dh-104-dove/d-14>, accessed 24 September 2021; and André Dillien, "Régistre 9O-9Q-9T-KAT", <https://doczz.fr/doc/71037/liste-des-immatriculations>, accessed 24 September 2021.

35 "Junkers Ju52/3m", <https://www.belgian-wings.be/junkers-ju52-3m>, accessed 22 September 2021.

36 "North American AT-6 Harvard/Texan", <https://www.belgian-wings.be/harvard-part-iv>, accessed 20 September 2021.

37 Correspondence with Daniel Brackx, 23 September 2021. <www.huisdervleugels.be/LtAvb/chapitre03.html>

38 "Aerial Visuals, Airframe Dossier", <https://www.aerialvisuals.ca/AirframeDossier.php?Serial=96250>, accessed 24 September 2021.

39 "Aircraft G-BSGC Data", <https://www.airport-data.com/aircraft/G-BSGC.html, accessed 24 September 2021.

40 "Stampe Vertongen SV-4B (Pre-War)", <https://www.belgian-wings.be/stampe-vertongen-sv-4b-pre-war>, accessed 24 September 2021.

41 "Les avions de la Force Publique du Congo"

42 Dillien, "Registre 9O-9Q-9T-KAT".

Chapter 7

1 "Belgian Congo (1908–1960)", <https://uca.edu/politicalscience/dadm-project/sub-saharan-africa-region/belgian-congo-1908-1960/>, accessed 15/09/2021. Also see, Zeilig, Renton, and Seddon, *The Congo: Plunder and Resistance*, p.69, and Bogumil Jewsiewicki, Kilola Lema, Jean-Luc Vellut, "Documents pour servir de l'histoire sociale du Zaire: grèves dans le Bas-Congo en 1945", *Etudes d'histoire africaine*, 1973, pp.155–188. Crawford Young, *Politics in the Congo: Decolonization and Independence* (New Jersey: Princeton University Press, 2015) pp.292–293.

2 Some sources put this figure at $25 per month. See, Crawford Young, "Background to Independence", p.36.

3 International Labour Office, "Les problèmes du travail en Afrique" (Geneva: International Labour Office, 1959), p.18.

4 Georges Brausch, *Belgian Administration in the Congo* (Oxford, OUP, 1961), p.11.

5 Brausch, *Belgian Administration in the Congo*, p.2.

6 International Labour Office, "Rapport sur les salaires dans la République du Congo" (Geneva, 1960), p.12, in *Brausch, Belgian Administration in the Congo*, p.2.

7 Brausch, *Belgian Administration in the Congo*, p.15.

8 Brausch, *Belgian Administration in the Congo*, p.20.

9 Didier Ndongala Mumbata, *Patrice Lumumba, Ahead of His Time* (London: Paragon Publishing, 2018), p.16.

10 Other associations were the *Union des Anciens Elèves des Frères Maristes* (UNELMA); the *Association des Anciens Elèves des Frères Chrètiens* (ASSANEF); and the *Anciens Elèves des Pères Jésuites*.

11 This association provided *évolués* with the means of discussing working conditions and wages. Ultimately, discussions would turn to equal pay for equal work and discrimination in the workplace. See, Colin Legum, "The Belgian Congo: Revolt of the Elite", *Africa South*, Vol.4, No.1, October-December 1959, pp.105–106.

12 Yolanda Covington-Ward, "Joseph Kasa-Vubu, ABAKO? and Performances of Kongo Nationalism in the Independence of Congo", *Journal of Black Studies*, Special issue: 1960s Africa in Historical Perspective, Vol.43, No.1, January 2012, p.74.

13 René Lemarchand, "The Bases of Nationalism among the Bakongo", *Africa: Journal of the International African Institute*, Vol.31, No.4, October 1961, p.346.

14 A. A. J. Van Bilsen, *Vers l'indépendance du Congo et du Ruanda-Urundi* (Kinshasa, Presses Universitaires, 1977), p.296.

15 "Excerpts from Prof. Van Bilsen's "Thirty Year Plan", in "Conflict in the Congo", *Africa Today*, Vol.7, No.5, September 1960, p.5.

16 "Excerpts from Prof. Van Bilsen's "Thirty Year Plan", p.5.

17 Jean Labrique, *Congo politique* (Leopoldville: Editions de l'Avenir, 1957), pp.251–264.

18 Benoît Verhaegen, *ABAKO, 1950–1960* (Brussels: Documents du CRISP, 1962), pp.37–44.

19 Verhaegen, *ABAKO, 1950–1960*, pp.37–44.

20 William Edward Burghardt Du Bois, "Fifth Pan-African Congress final resolution", October 1945, W. E. B. Du Bois Papers (MS 312). Special Collections and University Archives, University of Massachusetts Amherst Libraries.

21 Emmanuel Kwaku Akeampong and Henry Louis Gates, Dictionary of African Biography (New York: OUP, 2012), p.526.

22 Akeampong and Gates, *Dictionary of African Biography*, p.526.

23 George M. Houser, "A Report on the All-African People's Conference Held in Accra, Ghana, December 8–13, 1958", *American Committee on Africa*, New York.

24 Patrice Lumumba, "Speech at Accra", <https://www.blackpast.org/global-african-history/1958-patrice-lumumba-speech-accra/>, accessed 14 May 2019.

25 Patrice Lumumba, *Speech at Accra*.

26 Patrice Lumumba, *Speech at Accra*.

27 Patrice Lumumba, *Speech at Accra*.

28 The CEREA sought the unity of the Kivu people and the CONAKAT was restricted to activities in Katanga.

29 Georges Nzongola-Ntalaja, *From Leopold to Kabila: A People's History* (London: Zed Books, 2002), pp.84–86.

30 Leo Zeilig, *Lumumba: Africa's Lost Leader* (London: Haus, 2008), p.70.

31 Colin Legum, *Congo Disaster* (Baltimore: Penguin Books, 1960), p.59.

32 A. Rubbens, "Political Awakening in the Congo", *Civilisations*, Vol.10, No.1, 1960, p.64.

33 Rubbens, *Political Awakening in the Congo*, p.74.

34 Jeanne M. Haskin, *The Tragic State of the Congo: from Decolonization to Dictatorship* (New York: Algora Publishing, 2005), pp.19–20.

35 Homer Bigart, "Lumumba Victor in Congo Voting", *New York Times*, 1 June 1960.

36 "Belgian Congo Threats Spur European's Exodus", *New York Times*, 2 June 1960.

37 "Rhodesia to Bolster Border", *New York Times*, 1 June 1960.

38 "Emergency Declared in Katanga", *The Times*, 14 June 1960.

39 Harry Gilroy, "Divisive Efforts Spread in Congo", *New York Times*, 14 June 1960.

40 "Tshombe, Moïse-Kapenda", *Biographie Belge d'Outre-Mer* (Brussels: Académie Royale des Sciences d'Outre-mer, Tome VII-A), pp.462–476.

41 Article 250 of the Fundamental Law of 19 May 1960.

42 "New Congo State to Enforce Unity", *The Times*, 28 June 1960.

43 Madeleine Kalb, *The Congo Cables: The Cold War in Africa – From Eisenhower to Kennedy* (London: Macmillan, 1982), p.3.

Chapter 8

1 Daniel Brackx and Jean-Pierre Sonck, *L'appui-feu de Baka* (Brussels, Editions de Krijger, 2007), p.9.

2 Sonck, *L'aviation légère*.

3 Sonck, *L'aviation légère*.

4 Brackx and Sonck, *L'appui-feu de Baka*, p.14.

5 Brackx and Sonck, *L'appui-feu de Baka*, p.15.

6 "Belgian Congo (1908–1960)".

7 Brackx and Sonck, *L'appui-feu de Baka*, p.15.

8 "Belgian Congo (1908–1960)".

9 Brackx and Sonck, *L'appui-feu de Baka*, pp.17–18.

10 Brackx and Sonck, *L'appui-feu de Baka*, p.20.

11 Brackx and Sonck, *L'appui-feu de Baka*, p.23.

12 Emmanuel Gerard and Bruce Kulick, *Death in the Congo: Murdering Patrice Lumumba* (Cambridge, Mass., Harvard University Press, 2015), p.163.

13 Hoskyns, *The Congo since Independence*, p.87.

14 Hoskyns, *The Congo since Independence*, p.87.

15 Hoskyns, *The Congo since Independence*, p.88.

16 Brackx and Sonck, *L'appui-feu de Baka*, p.23.

17 Edgerton, *The Troubled Heart of Africa: A History of the Congo*, p.186.

18 Edgerton, *The Troubled Heart of Africa: A History of the Congo*, p.189.

19 "Army to be Commanded by Congolese", *The Times*, 9 July 1960.

20 Larry Devlin, *Chief of Station, Congo* (New York: Public Affairs, 2008), introduction, xiii–xv.

21 Edgerton, *The Troubled Heart of Africa: A History of the Congo*, p.188.
22 The 15th Transport Wing used around 15 Fairchild C-119s, two Douglas DC-4s, and three DC-6s to be used in the operations, and SABENA was also to play a role by providing five Boeing 707s, eight Douglas DC-7s and 12 DC-6s.
23 Edward R. Kantowitz, *The World in the Twentieth Century Vol.2: Coming Apart, Coming Together* (Cambridge: William B. Eerdmans Publishing Company, 2000), p.273.
24 "US Mission at the UN", Cable No.1137 to the State Department in Kalb, *Congo Cables*, p.15.
25 "From a letter to Dag Hammarskjöld, U.N. Secretary-General, August 14, 1960", https://www.marxists.org/subject/africa/lumumba/1960/08/umgensec.htm, accessed 19 October 2021.
26 "Questions relating to the situation in the Republic of the Congo (Leopoldville)", The Yearbook of the United Nations, 1960, Part 1, Chapter VII, p.52.
27 "Questions relating to the situation in the Republic of the Congo (Leopoldville)", p.54.
28 *New York Times*, 29 July 1960, in Kalb, *Congo Cables*, p.19.
29 Daniel L. Haulman, "Congolese Mercy Airlift", *Air Mobility Command Museum*, (date unknown) available at <https://amcmuseum.org/history/congolese-mercy-airlift/>, accessed 1 July 2019.
30 Kalb, *Congo Cables*, p.19.
31 Luc De Vos, Emmanuel Gérard, Jules Gérard-Libois, and Philippe Raxhorn, *Les secrets de l'affaire Lumumba* (Bruxelles: Editions Racine, 2005), p.62.
32 Brackx & Sonck, L'appui-feu de Baka, pp.64–65.
33 Brackx & Sonck, L'appui-feu de Baka, p.67.
34 Brackx & Sonck, *L'appui-feu de Baka*, p.73.
35 Brackx & Sonck, *L'appui-feu de Baka*, p.91.

About the Author

Dr. Stephen Rookes works for the French Air Force as a researcher and lecturer at the *Centre de Recherche de l'Armée de l'air et de l'espace* (CREA) in Salon-de-Provence, France. Originally from Devon in the UK, but now a French national, Stephen Rookes is the author of four books published by Helion, and the author of peer-reviewed articles in English and in French.